CROCHET
Year-Round Scraps Aplenty™

General Information

Many of the products used in this pattern book can be purchased from local craft, fabric and variety stores, or from the Annie's Attic Needlecraft Catalog (*see Customer Service information on page 56*).

Rose Garden Accessories

Designs by Sandy Abbate

SKILL LEVEL

INTERMEDIATE

FINISHED SIZES
Barrette: 1¾ x 3¾ inches
Button Cover: 1½ inches in diameter

MATERIALS
❏ Crochet cotton size 10:
    50 yds each pink, lavender,
    yellow, blue and green
❏ Size 8/1.50mm steel crochet
    hook or size needed to
    obtain gauge
❏ Tapestry needle
❏ 2½-inch-long barrette back
❏ 3 (¾-inch) covered button backs
❏ 6 (⅛-inch) pearls
❏ Craft glue

GAUGE
Rose = 1¼ inches in diameter

INSTRUCTIONS
ROSE
Make 2 each pink, lavender & yellow.
Rnd 1: Ch 4, sl st in first ch to form ring, ch 1, [sc in ring, ch 4] 5 times, join with sl st in beg sc. *(5 ch-4 sps)*

Rnd 2 (WS): (Sc, hdc, 3 dc, hdc, sc) in each ch-4 sp around, **do not join**. *(5 petals)*

Rnd 3: Working in front of petals of last rnd, sc around post *(see Stitch Guide)* of first unworked sc of rnd 1, ch 5, [sc around post of next unworked sc of rnd 1, ch 5] around, join with sl st in beg sc. *(5 ch-5 sps)*

Rnd 4: (Sc, hdc, 5 dc, hdc, sc) in each ch-5 sp around, join with sl st in beg sc. Fasten off.

Leaf Cluster
Make 6.
With green, ch 14, *sc in 2nd ch from hook, hdc in next ch, dc in next ch, tr in each of next 3 chs, dc in next ch, hdc in next ch, sc in next ch, sl st in next ch*, [ch 11, rep between *] twice, sl st in each of last 3 chs of ch-14. Fasten off.

Forget-Me-Not
Make 6.
With blue, ch 4, sl st in first ch to form ring, ch 1, [sc in ring, ch 3] 6 times, join with sl st in beg sc. Fasten off.

With tapestry needle and yellow, work French knot *(see illustration)* in the center of each forget-me-not.

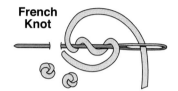

French Knot

Finishing
1. Glue 1 Leaf Cluster at each end of barrette and 1 in the center on either edge.
2. Glue yellow Rose at center of barrette and 1 pink Rose and 1 lavender Rose on opposite sides.
3. Glue 1 Forget-Me-Not on center leaf of each Leaf Cluster.
4. Glue 1 pearl to center of each Rose.
5. Glue 1 Leaf Cluster to edge of each covered button back and 1 Rose over center of each covered button back.
6. Glue 1 Forget-Me-Not to center leaf of each Leaf Cluster and 1 pearl to center of each Rose. ❑❑

Vineyard Wine Caddy & Coasters

Designs by Sandy Abbate

SKILL LEVEL
BEGINNER

FINISHED SIZES
Caddy: 5 inches in diameter x 6 inches tall
Coaster: 5 inches in diameter

MATERIALS
- ❑ Medium (worsted) weight yarn:
  3 oz/150 yds/85g deep crimson
  1 oz/50 yds/28g each violet and woodsy green
- ❑ Size F/5/3.75mm crochet hook or size needed to obtain gauge
- ❑ Tapestry needle
- ❑ 1⅔ yds ⅛ inch gold ribbon

GAUGE
9 dc = 2 inches, 5 dc rnds = 2 inches

INSTRUCTIONS
COASTER
Make 2.
First Grape
With violet, ch 3, 11 hdc in 3rd ch *(first 2 chs count as first hdc)* from hook, join with sl st in 2nd ch of beg ch-2. Fasten off. *(12 hdc)*

Second Grape
Rep First Grape, **do not fasten off**, sl st in **back lp** *(see Stitch Guide)* of joining of First Grape. Fasten off.

Third Grape
With violet, ch 3, 9 hdc in 3rd ch from hook *(first 2 chs count as first hdc)*, sl st in 2nd st from joining on First grape, work 1 hdc in same ch on this grape, sl st in 2nd st from joining on Second grape, hdc in same ch on this grape, join with sl st in 2nd ch of beg ch-2. Fasten off.

Vine
Rnd 1(RS): Join woodsy green with sl st in sp between Grapes, ch 1, *(sc, ch 9, sc) in sp between Grapes, ch 6, working in back lps, sk next 4 hdc, (sc, ch 6, sc) in next hdc, ch 6, rep from * twice, join with sl st in beg sc. Fasten off.

Rnd 2 (RS): Join woodsy green with sl st in any ch-9 sp, ch 1, sc in same ch sp, *ch 4, [sc in next ch-6 sp, ch 3] 3 times**, sc in next ch-9 sp, rep from * around, ending last rep at **, join with sl st in beg sc. Fasten off. *(12 ch-4 sps)*

Rnd 3 (RS): Join deep crimson with sl st in any ch-4 sp, ch 3 *(counts as first dc throughout)*, 3 dc in same ch sp, dc in next sc, [4 dc in next ch-4 sp, dc in next sc] around, join with sl st in 3rd ch of beg ch-3. Fasten off. *(60 dc)*

Rnd 4 (RS): Join violet with sl st in any dc, ch 1, **sc dec** *(see Stitch Guide)* in first 2 sts, ch 3, [sc dec in next 2 sts, ch 3] around, join with sl st in beg sc dec. Fasten off.

Cut 8-inch length of ribbon. Tie in bow around any dc of rnd 3.

WINE CADDY
Rnd 1 (RS): Beg at bottom with deep crimson, ch 4, 15 dc in 4th ch from hook *(first 3 chs count as first dc)*, join with sl st in 3rd ch of beg ch-3. *(16 dc)*

Rnd 2: Ch 3, dc in same st, 2 dc in each st around, join with sl st in 3rd ch of beg ch-3. *(32 dc)*

Rnd 3: Ch 3, 2 dc in next dc, [dc in next dc, 2 dc in next dc] around, join with sl st in 3rd ch of beg ch-3. *(48 dc)*

Rnd 4: Working in back lps for this rnd only, ch 3, dc in each st around, join with sl st in top of beg ch-3.

Rnd 5: Ch 3, dc in each dc around, join with sl st in 3rd ch of beg ch-3, pull up lp of woodsy green, drop deep crimson to WS, **do not fasten off**.

Rnd 6: With woodsy green, ch 3, working in front of beg ch, dc in dc before beg ch *(cross st)*, [sk next dc, dc in next dc, working in front of last dc, dc in dc just sk *(cross st)*] around, join with sl st in 3rd ch of beg ch-3. Fasten off woodsy green. *(24 cross sts)*

Rnd 7: Pull up lp of deep crimson and sl st in joining, ch 3, dc in each dc around, join with sl st in 3rd ch of beg ch-3. *(48 dc)*

Rnds 8–13: Ch 3, dc in each dc around, join with sl st in 3rd ch of beg ch-3.

Rnds 14–17: Rep rnds 5–8. At end of last rnd, fasten off.

Rnd 18: Join violet with sl st in any dc, ch 1, sc dec in first 2 dc, ch 3, [sc dec in next 2 dc, ch 3] around, join with sl st in beg sc dec. Fasten off.

Bottom Trim

Rnd 1: Join deep crimson in rem unworked lps of rnd 3, ch 3, dc in next st, 2 dc in next st, [dc in each of next 2 sts, 2 dc in next st] around, join with sl st in 3rd ch of beg ch-3. *(64 dc)*

Rnd 2: Ch 3, dc in each of next 2 sts, 2 dc in next st, [dc in each of next 3 sts, 2 sc in next st] around, join with sl st in 3rd ch of beg ch-3. Fasten off. *(80 dc)*

Rnd 3: Join violet with sl st in any dc, ch 1, sc dec in first 2 dc, ch 3, [sc dec in next 2 dc, ch 3] around, join with sl st in beg sc dec. Fasten off.

APPLIQUÉS
Leaf Group

With woodsy green, ch 10, *sc in 2nd ch from hook, hdc in next ch, dc in next ch, hdc in next ch, sc in next ch, sl st in next ch**, ch 7, rep from * across, ending 2nd rep at **, sc in each of last 3 chs of beg ch-10. Leaving long end, fasten off.

Grape
Make 9.

With violet, ch 3, 11 hdc in 3rd ch from hook, join with sl st in 2nd ch of beg ch-2. Leaving long end, fasten off.

Finishing

1. Grapes and Leaf Group are sewn to Caddy between rnds 5–14. Sew first Grape over rnd 5, 2 Grapes centered over previous Grape, 3 Grapes centered above previous Grapes and sew rem 2 Grapes centered above previous Grapes leaving center sp free.

2. Sew stem of Leaf Group in sp between last 2 Grapes at top, and Leaves above.

3. Cut 2 lengths of gold ribbon each 22 inches. Weave first length over and under sts of rnd 4, gather slightly, tie ends in bow. Weave 2nd length over and under sts of rnd 17, tie ends in bow. ❏❏

Itzy-Bitzy Bear

Design by Sandy Abbate

SKILL LEVEL
INTERMEDIATE

FINISHED SIZE
4 inches tall

MATERIALS
- ❑ Crochet cotton size 10:
  100 yds maize
  25 yds each blue and green
- ❑ 2 yds brown 6-strand embroidery floss
- ❑ Size 7/1.65mm steel crochet hook or size needed to obtain gauge
- ❑ Tapestry needle
- ❑ ½ yd ⅛-inch-wide red satin ribbon
- ❑ Small amount polyester fiberfill
- ❑ Blusher

GAUGE
10 sc = 1 inch, 9 sc rows = 1 inch

PATTERN NOTE
Do not join rounds unless otherwise stated; mark first stitch of each round with safety pin or other small marker.

INSTRUCTIONS
BEAR
Head
Rnd 1: With maize, ch 2, 6 sc in 2nd ch from hook, **do not join** (see Pattern Note). (6 sc)

Rnd 2: 2 sc in each st around. (12 sc)

Rnd 3: [Sc in next st, 2 sc in next st] around. (18 sc)

Rnd 4: [Sc in each of next 2 sts, 2 sc in next st] around. (24 sc)

Rnds 5 & 6: Sc in each st around.

Rnd 7: 2 sc in each of first 4 sts, sc in each st around. (28 sc)

Rnds 8 & 9: Sc in each st around.

Rnd 10: [**Sc dec** (see Stitch Guide) in next 2 sts] 4 times, sc in each st around. (24 sc)

Rnd 11: [Sc in each of next 2 sts, sc dec in next 2 sts] around. (18 sc)

Rnd 12: [Sc in next st, sc dec in next 2 sts] around. (12 sc)

Body
Rnd 13: [Sc in next st, 2 sc in next st] around. (18 sc)

Rnd 14: [Sc in each of next 2 sts, 2 sc in next st] around. (24 sc)

Rnd 15: [Sc in each of next 3 sts, 2 sc in next st] around. (30 sc)

Rnds 16–22: Sc in each st around.

Rnd 23: [Sc in each of next 3 sts, sc dec in next 2 sts] around. (24 sc)

Rnd 24: [Sc in each of next 2 sts, sc dec in next 2 sts] around. (18 sc)

Rnd 25: [Sc in next st, sc dec in next 2 sts] around. (12 sc)

Stuff Head and body.

Rnd 26: [Sc dec in next 2 sts] around, join with sl st in beg sc dec. Leaving long end, fasten off.

Thread end into tapestry needle, weave through sts of last rnd, pull tightly to close and fasten off.

Arm
Make 2.
Rnds 1 & 2: Beg at top of arm, rep rnds 1 and 2 of Head. *(12 sc)*

Rnds 3–12: Sc in each st around. Stuff arm lightly.

Rnd 13: [Sc dec in next 2 sts] around, join with sl st in beg sc. Leaving a 12-inch end, fasten off.

Close opening same as for Body.

Leg
Make 2.
Rnds 1–3: Beg at foot, rep rnds 1–3 of Head. *(18 sc)*

Rnds 4–6: Sc in each st around.

Rnd 7: [Sc dec in next 2 sts] 4 times, sc in each st around. *(14 sc)*

Rnds 8–15: Sc in each st around. Stuff leg lightly.

Rnd 16: [Sc dec in next 2 sts] around, join with sl st in beg sc dec. Leaving a 12-inch end, fasten off.

Close opening same as for Body.

Ear
Make 2.
Row 1: With maize, ch 5, sc in 2nd ch from hook and in each of next 3 chs, turn. *(4 sc)*

Row 2: Ch 1, 2 sc in first st, sc in each of next 2 sts, 2 sc in last st, turn. *(6 sc)*

Row 3: Ch 1, sc in each sc across, turn.

Row 4: Ch 1, sc dec in first 2 sts, sc in each of next 2 sts, sc dec in last 2 sts. Fasten off.

HAT
Hat Ribbing
Row 1: With blue, ch 6, sc in 2nd ch from hook and in each ch across, turn. *(5 sc)*

Rows 2–24: Working in **back lps** *(see Stitch Guide)* only, ch 1, sc in each sc across, turn. At end of last row, **do not turn, do not fasten off.**

Crown
Row 1: Working across long edge, ch 1, sc in end of each row across, turn. *(24 sc)*

Row 2: Ch 3 *(counts as first dc throughout)*, dc in each of next 3 sts, ch 4, sk next 4 sts, dc in each of next 8 sts, ch 4, sk next 4 sts, dc in each of last 4 sts, turn.

Row 3: Ch 3, dc in each dc and 4 dc in each ch-4 sp across, turn. *(24 dc)*

Row 4: Ch 3, dc in each dc across. Fasten off.

Thread tapestry needle with 20-inch length of blue. Beg at bottom of Hat, sew back seam to top, weave thread through sts of last row and pull tightly to close, fasten off.

Pompom
Wrap green 30 times around your thumb. Remove thread from thumb and tie securely at center with separate piece of green. Trim and tie to top of Hat.

Finishing
1. Embroider face, paws and toes as shown in photo, using 6 strands floss.
2. Sew on Ears, Arms and Legs.
3. Place Hat on Head and poke Ears through holes.
4. Apply blusher to cheeks, inside of Ears, and bottoms of paws and feet.
5. Cut satin ribbon in half; tie 1 length into bow around neck and 1 length in bow around ankle. ❏❏

Charlie Chimp

Design by Barbara Anderson

FINISHED SIZE
9 inches tall, sitting

MATERIALS
- ❑ Medium (worsted) weight yarn:
  4 oz/200 yds/113g brown
  1 oz/50 yds/28g each peach,
  turquoise and yellow
  ½ oz/25 yds/14g off-white
- ❑ Size F/5/3.75mm crochet hook
  or size needed to obtain gauge
- ❑ Stitch marker
- ❑ Tapestry needle
- ❑ Sewing needle
- ❑ Sewing thread
- ❑ Black embroidery floss
- ❑ 2 black size 12mm animal
  eyes with washers
- ❑ 12-inch chenille stem
- ❑ ½ x 1 inch strip
  hook-and-loop tape
- ❑ Polyester fiberfill

GAUGE
9 sc = 2 inches, 9 sc rows = 2 inches

PATTERN NOTES
Do not join rounds unless otherwise stated. Mark first stitch of each round.

When changing colors *(see Stitch Guide)*, always change in last stitch made and drop yarn to wrong side of work.

Use separate skein or ball of yarn for each color section.

Do not carry yarn across from 1 section to another. Fasten off colors at end of each color section.

SPECIAL STITCH
Cluster (cl): Yo, insert hook in next st, yo, pull lp through, yo, pull through 2 lps on hook, [yo, insert hook in same st, yo, pull lp through, yo, pull through 2 lps on hook] twice, yo, pull through all lps on hook.

INSTRUCTIONS

CHIMP
Head
Rnd 1: Starting at **muzzle**, with peach, ch 4, 2 sc in 2nd ch from hook, 2 sc in next ch, 4 sc in end ch, working on opposite side of ch, for **center bottom**, 2 sc in each of last 2 chs, **do not join** *(see Pattern Notes)*. *(12 sc)*

Rnd 2: [2 sc in next st, sc in next st] around. *(18 sc)*

NOTE: *To move first st, sc or sl st in first st.*

Rnd 3: Sc in each of first 14 sts leaving rem sts unworked, move marker *(first st has been moved)*.

Rnd 4: Sc in each of first 4 sts, 2 sc in each of next 10 sts, sc in each of last 4 sts, join with sl st in beg sc. Fasten off. *(28 sc)*

Rnd 5: Join brown with sl st in first st, ch 2 *(counts as first hdc)*, hdc in each of next 10 sts changing to peach *(see Pattern Notes)* in last st made, 2 hdc in each of next 6 sts changing to brown, hdc in each of last 11 sts, join with sl st in 2nd ch of beg ch-2. *(34 hdc)*

Rnd 6: Ch 2, hdc in each of next 4 sts, 2 hdc in each of next 5 sts, 2 hdc in next st changing to peach, hdc in each of next 4 sts, hdc in next st changing to brown, hdc in each of next 2 sts changing to peach, hdc in each of next 4 sts, hdc in next st changing to brown, 2 hdc in each of next 6 sts, hdc in each of last 5 sts, join with sl st in 2nd ch of beg ch-2. Fasten off peach. *(46 hdc)*

Rnd 7: Ch 2, hdc in each of next 17 sts, [2 hdc in next st, hdc in next st] 5 times, 2 hdc in next st, hdc in each of last 17 sts, join with sl st in 2nd ch of beg ch-2. *(52 hdc)*

Rnd 8: Ch 2, hdc in each st around, join with sl st in 2nd ch of beg ch-2. Sl st in next st.

Rnd 9: Ch 2, [**hdc dec** *(see Stitch Guide)* in next 2 sts] 4 times, hdc in each of next 35 sts, [hdc dec in next 2 sts] 4 times, join with sl st in 2nd ch of beg ch-2. *(44 hdc)*

Attach eyes with washers 1¾ inches apart over rnd 6.

Rnd 10: Ch 2, hdc in each st around, join with sl st in 2nd ch of beg ch-2. Sl st in next st.

Rnd 11: Ch 2, hdc in each st around, join with sl st in 2nd ch of beg ch-2.

Rnd 12: Ch 2, hdc in each st around, join with sl st in 2nd ch of beg ch-2. Sl st in next st.

Rnd 13: Ch 2, hdc in each of next 3 sts, hdc dec in next 2 sts, [hdc in each of next 4 sts, hdc dec in next 2 sts] 5 times, hdc in each of next 6 sts, hdc dec in last 2 sts, join with sl st in 2nd ch of beg ch-2. *(37 hdc)*

Rnd 14: Ch 2, hdc in each st around, join with sl st in 2nd ch of beg ch-2. Sl st in next st. Stuff.

Rnd 15: Ch 2, [hdc dec in next 2 sts, hdc in next st] around, join with sl st in 2nd ch of beg ch-2. *(25 hdc)*

Rnd 16: Ch 2, hdc in each st around, join with sl st in 2nd ch of beg ch-2. Sl st in next st.

Rnd 17: Ch 2, [hdc dec in next 2 sts] 12 times, join with sl st in 2nd ch of beg ch-2. Stuff. *(13 hdc)*

Rnd 18: Ch 2, [hdc dec in next 2 sts] 6 times, join with sl st in 2nd ch of beg ch-2. Leaving long end for sewing, fasten off.
Sew opening closed.

Nose & Mouth
With black floss, embroider 2 lazy daisy sts *(see illustration)* on rnd 2 for nostrils and embroider mouth line in outline st *(see illustration)* between rnds 2 and 3 stitching over rnd 3 on edges as shown in photo.

Lazy Daisy Stitch

Outline Stitch

Brow

With 2 strands peach held tog, ch 20 leaving long end for sewing, fasten off.

Position ch around each eye section. Sew **back lps** (see Stitch Guide) of ch to Head, sew front lps between eyes to Head. Sew front lps of 3 chs to inside under each eye.

Ear
Make 2.

Row 1: With 2 strands peach held tog, ch 3 (first 2 chs count as first hdc), 6 hdc in 3rd ch from hook, turn. (7 hdc)

Row 2: Ch 1, 2 sc in each st across. Fasten off. (14 sc)

Sew ears to rnd 8 on Head 3½ inches apart across top of Head.

Body

Rnd 1: Starting at neck, with brown, ch 24, sl st in first ch to form ring, ch 1, sc in each ch around, join with sl st in first sc. (24 sc)

Rnd 2: Ch 2, hdc in each st around, join with sl st in 2nd ch of beg ch-2.

Rnd 3: Ch 2, hdc in each st around, join with sl st in 2nd ch of beg ch-2. Sl st in next st.

Rnds 4–6: Rep rnds 2 and 3 alternately, ending with rnd 2.

Rnd 7: Ch 2, hdc in each of next 6 sts, [2 hdc in next st, hdc in next st] 5 times, 2 hdc in next st, hdc in each of last 6 sts, join with sl st in 2nd ch of beg ch-2. (30 hdc)

Rnds 8 & 9: Rep rnds 3 and 2.

Rnd 10: Ch 2, [2 hdc in next st, hdc in next st] twice, 2 hdc in next st, hdc in each of next 19 sts, [2 hdc in next st, hdc in next st] twice, 2 hdc in last st, join with sl st in 2nd ch of beg ch-2. Sl st in next st. (36 hdc)

Rnds 11–16: Rep rnds 2 and 3 alternately.

Rnd 17: Ch 2, hdc in next st, hdc dec in next 2 sts, [hdc in each of next 2 sts, hdc dec in next 2 sts] around, join with sl st in top of beg ch-2. (27 hdc)

Rnd 18: Ch 2, hdc dec in next 2 sts, [hdc in next st, hdc dec in next 2 sts] around, join with sl st in 2nd ch of beg ch-2. (18 hdc)

Rnd 19: Ch 2, [hdc dec in next 2 sts] 8 times, hdc in last st, join with sl

st in top of beg ch-2. Leaving long end for sewing, fasten off. Stuff. Sew opening closed.

Sew bottom of rnds 8–13 of Head to rnd 1 on body.

Leg
Make 2.

Rnd 1: Starting at hip, with brown, ch 2, 8 sc in 2nd ch from hook, join with sl st in first sc. (8 sc)

Rnd 2: Ch 2, hdc in same st, 2 hdc in each st around, join with sl st in 2nd ch of beg ch-2. (16 hdc)

Rnd 3: Ch 2, [2 hdc in next st, hdc in each of next 2 sts] around, join with sl st in 2nd ch of beg ch-2. (21 hdc)

Rnd 4: Ch 2, hdc in each st around, join with sl st in 2nd ch of beg ch-2. Sl st in next st.

Rnd 5: Ch 2, hdc in each st around, join with sl st in 2nd ch of beg ch-2.

Rnds 6 & 7: Rep rnds 4 and 5.

Rnd 8: Ch 2, hdc dec in next 2 sts, hdc in each of next 16 sts, hdc dec in last 2 sts, join with sl st in 2nd ch of beg ch-2. (19 hdc)

Rnd 9: Ch 2, hdc in each st around, join with sl st in 2nd ch of beg ch-2. Sl st in next st.

Rnd 10: Ch 2, [hdc dec in next 2 sts] twice, hdc in each of next 4 sts, 2 hdc in each of next 2 sts, hdc in each of next 4 sts, [hdc dec in next 2 sts] twice, join with sl st in 2nd ch of beg ch-2. Stuff lightly. (17 hdc)

Rnd 11: Ch 2, hdc dec in next 2 sts, hdc in each of next 5 sts, 2 hdc in each of next 2 sts, hdc in each of next 5 sts, hdc dec in last 2 sts, join with sl st in 2nd ch of beg ch-2. Sl st in next st. (17 hdc)

Rnd 12: Ch 2, hdc dec in next 2 sts, hdc in each of next 5 sts, 2 hdc in each of next 2 sts, hdc in each of next 5 sts, hdc dec in last 2 sts, join with sl st in 2nd ch of beg ch-2.

Rnd 13: Ch 2, hdc in each st around, join with sl st in 2nd ch of beg ch-2. Sl st in next st.

Rnd 14: Ch 2, hdc in same st, 2 hdc in next st, hdc in each of next 4 sts, [hdc dec in next 2 sts] 3 times, hdc in each of next 4 sts, 2 hdc in last st, join with sl st in 2nd ch of beg ch-2.

Rnds 15 & 16: Rep rnds 4 and 5. At end of last rnd, fasten off.

Rnd 17: For **foot**, sk first st, join peach with sc in next st, sc in each st around, **do not join.** (17 sc)

Rnd 18: Sc in each of first 6 sts, 2 sc in each of next 5 sts, sc in each of last 6 sts. (22 sc)

Rnd 19: Sc in each of first 8 sts, 2 sc in each of next 6 sts, sc in each of last 8 sts. Sc in first st. (28 sc)

Rnd 20: Sc in each st around. Sc in first st.

Rnd 21: Sc in each of first 10 sts, [**cl** (see Special Stitch), ch 1, sc in next st] 4 times, sc in each of last 10 sts.

Rnd 22: [Sc dec (see Stitch Guide) in next 2 sts] twice, sc in each of next 6 sts, [sc in next ch, sc in next st] 4 times, sc in each of next 6 sts, [sc dec in next 2 sts] twice. (24 sc)

Rnd 23: [Sc dec in next 2 sts] around. (12 sc)

Rnd 24: Sc in each st around, join with sl st in beg sc. Leaving long end for sewing, fasten off.

Stuff. Sew opening closed lengthwise.

Sew rnds 1–8 of Legs to sides of Body 1 inch apart across back over rnds 11–16.

Large Toe
Make 2.

Rnd 1: With peach, ch 4, sc in 2nd ch from hook, sc in next ch, 2 sc in end ch, working on opposite side of ch, sc in each of last 2 chs. (6 sc)

Rnd 2: Sc in each of first 3 sts, ch 3 leaving last 3 sts unworked, join with sl st in first sc. (3 sc, 3 chs)

Rnd 3: Ch 1, sc in each st and in each ch around. (6 sc)

Rnd 4: Sc in each of first 4 sts, sc dec in last 2 sts. (5 sc)

Rnd 5: Sc in each st around. Fasten off. Stuff.

Sew opening closed.

Sew unworked sts of rnd 2 to inside of foot over rnds 20 and 21.

Arm
Make 2.

Rnd 1: Starting at shoulder, with brown, ch 2, 6 sc in 2nd ch from hook, join with sl st in beg sc. (6 sc)

Rnd 2: Ch 2, hdc in same st, 2 hdc in each st around, join with sl st in 2nd ch of beg ch-2. (12 hdc)

Rnd 3: Ch 2, hdc in same st, hdc in next st, [2 hdc in next st, hdc in next st] around, join with sl st in 2nd ch of beg ch-2. *(18 hdc)*

Rnd 4: Ch 2, hdc in each st around, join with sl st in 2nd ch of beg ch-2. Sl st in next st.

Rnd 5: Ch 2, hdc in each st around, join with sl st in 2nd ch of beg ch-2.

Rnds 6 & 7: Rep rnds 4 and 5.

Rnd 8: Ch 2, hdc dec in next 2 sts, hdc in each of next 13 sts, hdc dec in last 2 sts, join with sl st in 2nd ch of beg ch-2. *(16 hdc)*

Rnd 9: Ch 2, hdc dec in next 2 sts, hdc in each of last 13 sts, join with sl st in 2nd ch of beg ch-2. Sl st in next st. *(15 hdc)*

Rnds 10 & 11: Ch 2, hdc dec in next 2 sts, hdc in each of next 4 sts, 2 hdc in each of next 2 sts, hdc in each of next 4 sts, hdc dec in last 2 sts, join with sl st in 2nd ch of beg ch-2. At end of last rnd, sl st in next st. **Do not stuff.** *(15 hdc)*

Rnds 12 & 13: Rep rnds 10 and 11.

Rnd 14: Ch 2, hdc in each st around, join with sl st in 2nd ch of beg ch-2. Fasten off.

Rnd 15: For **hand**, join peach with sc in first st, sc in each st around. *(15 sc)*

Rnd 16: Sc in each st around. Sc in first st.

Rnd 17: Sc in each st around.

Rnds 18 & 19: Rep rnds 16 and 17.

Rnd 20: Sc in each st around. For **left arm only**, join with sl st in first sc. Fasten off.

Cut chenille stem in half. Fold one end under ½ inch, insert in arm with folded end even with rnd 20, stuff around stem.

Row 21: Working in rows, through both thicknesses, for **right arm**, [cl in next st, sc in next st] 4 times. Leaving long end for sewing, fasten off.

Row 21: Working in rows, through both thicknesses, for **left arm**, join peach with sl st in 7th st on rnd 20, [cl in next st, sc in next st] 4 times. Leaving long end for sewing, fasten off.

Sew chs on ends of cl and sc to sts on rnd 20.

Thumb
Make 2.
Rnds 1–5: Rep same rnds as Large Toe.

Sew unworked sts of rnd 2 to inside of Arm over rnds 13–15.

Flatten rnds 1–3 of Arm, sew slightly cupped over rnds 2–4 on sides of Body 1¾ inches apart across back.

SHIRT
Row 1: Starting at neckline, with turquoise, ch 35, sc in 2nd ch from hook and in each ch across, turn. *(34 sc)*

Row 2: Working this row in front lps only, ch 3 *(counts as first dc)*, dc in each of next 4 sts, 2 dc in each of next 6 sts, dc in each of next 12 sts, 2 dc in each of next 6 sts, dc in each of last 5 sts, turn. *(46 dc)*

Row 3: Ch 3, dc in same st, dc in each of next 4 sts, [for **armhole**, ch 10, sk next 12 sts]; dc in each of next 12 sts; rep between [ ], dc in each of next 4 sts, 2 dc in last st, turn. *(24 sts, 20 chs)*

Row 4: Ch 3, dc in each st and in each ch across, turn. *(44 dc)*

Row 5: Ch 3, dc in each of next 12 sts, [2 dc in next st, dc in next st] 9 times, dc in each of last 13 sts, turn. *(53 dc)*

Row 6: Ch 3, dc in each st across, turn. Fasten off.

Row 7: Join turquoise with sc in end of row 1, 2 sc in end of each of next 5 rows, working in back lps, 2 sc in first st on row 6, sc in each of next 51 sts, 2 sc in last st, 2 sc in end of each of next 5 rows, sc in end of row 1. Fasten off.

Sleeves
Rnd 1: Join turquoise with sl st in 5th ch on row 3, ch 3, dc in each of next 5 chs, 2 dc in end of row 3, dc in each of next 12 sts, 2 dc in end of row 3, dc in each of last 4 chs, join with sl st in top of beg ch-3. *(26 dc)*

Rnd 2: Ch 3, dc in each st around, join with sl st in top of beg ch-3.

Rnd 3: Working this rnd in back lps only, ch 1, sc in each st around, join with sl st in beg sc. Fasten off.

Rep in other armhole.

Sew hook-and-loop tape on back of Shirt.

BANANA
Rnd 1: With off-white, ch 2, 6 sc in 2nd ch from hook. *(6 sc)*

Rnd 2: 2 sc in each st around. *(12 sc)*

Rnds 3–10: Sc in each st around. Stuff.

Rnd 11: Sc in first st, 2 sc in each of next 3 sts, sc in each of next 2 sts, [sc dec in next 2 sts] 3 times. *(12 sc)*

Rnds 12–21: Sc in each st around.

Rnd 22: [Sc dec in next 2 sts] around, join with sl st in first sc. Leaving long end for sewing, fasten off. Stuff.

Sew opening closed.

Peel
Rnd 1: With yellow, ch 2, 6 sc in 2nd ch from hook. *(6 sc)*

Rnd 2: Working this rnd in back lps only, sc in each st around.

Rnd 3: 2 sc in each st around. *(12 sc)*

Rnd 4: For **sections**, [sl st in next st, ch 23, sc in 2nd ch from hook, hdc in next ch, dc in next ch, tr in each of next 19 chs, sk next st on rnd 3] 6 times, sl st in last st. Fasten off.

Sew ends of rows on 2 peel sections tog forming 1 piece; rep with rem sections for a total of 3 pieces.

Sew long edges of peel pieces tog halfway up as shown in photo.

Place Banana inside peel. ❑❑

Dressed-Up Doggies

Designs by Vicki Blizzard

SKILL LEVEL

BEGINNER

FINISHED SIZE
Neck: 12 inches *(adjustable)*

MATERIALS
- ❑ Medium (worsted) weight yarn:
  2 oz/100 yds/57g white
  ½ oz/25 yds/14g each red
  and royal blue for Sailor
  Collar
  2 oz/100 yds/57g desired
  color for Bow Tie
- ❑ Size H/8/5mm crochet hook or
  size needed to obtain gauge
- ❑ Tapestry needle
- ❑ Sewing needle
- ❑ Sewing thread
- ❑ 1-inch square hook-and-loop
  tape for each collar
- ❑ 2 (⅝-inch) red star-shaped
  buttons for Sailor Collar

GAUGE
4 sts = 1 inch, 4 sc rows = 1 inch

INSTRUCTIONS

BOW TIE
Neck Band

Row 1: Ch 5, sc in 2nd ch from hook
and in each ch across, turn. *(4 sc)*

Row 2: Ch 1, sc in each sc across,
turn.

Next rows: Rep row 2 until neck band
wraps comfortably around dog's
neck, allowing for a 2 inch overlap.
At end of last row, fasten off.

Sew hook piece of tape to 1 end of neck
band. Sew loop piece to opposite side
of opposite end of neck band.

Bow

Row 1: Ch 5, sc in 2nd ch from hook
and in each ch across, turn. *(4 sc)*

Rows 2–4: Ch 1, sc in each sc across,
turn.

Row 5: Ch 1, 2 sc in first st, sc in
each st across with 2 sc in last st,
turn. *(6 sc)*

Row 6: Ch 1, sc in each sc across,
turn.

Rows 7–10: Rep rows 5 and 6 alternately twice. *(10 sc on each of last
2 rows)*

Rows 11 & 12: Ch 1, sc in each st
across, turn.

Row 13: Ch 1, **sc dec** *(see Stitch Guide)*
in first 2 sts, sc in each st across with
sc dec in last 2 sts, turn. *(8 sts)*

Row 14: Ch 1, sc in each sc across,
turn.

Rows 15–18: Rep rows 13 and 14
alternately twice. *(4 sts on each of
last 2 rows)*

Rows 19–26: Ch 1, sc in each st
across, turn.

Rows 27–44: Rep rows 5–22. At end
of last row, leaving 12-inch end for
sewing, fasten off.

With tapestry needle and 12-inch end,
whipstitch rows 1 and 44 tog. Fold Bow
so that narrowest rows are at center
and widest rows are at each end.

Knot

Row 1: Ch 5, sc in 2nd ch from hook
and in each ch across, turn. *(4 sc)*

Rows 2–10: Ch 1, sc in each sc across, turn. At end of last row, leaving 12-inch end for sewing, fasten off. Wrap knot around center of Bow. With tapestry needle and 12-inch end, whipstitch ends of knot tog. Sew Bow to end of Neck Band.

SAILOR COLLAR
Neck Band
Row 1: With red, ch 5, sc in 2nd ch from hook and in each ch across, turn. *(4 sc)*

Row 2: Ch 1, sc in each sc across, turn.

Next rows: Rep row 2 until neck band wraps comfortably around dog's neck, allowing for a 2-inch overlap. At end of last row, fasten off.

Collar
Row 1 (RS): Working in end of rows on Neck Band, join white with sl st in end of 11th row from center of Neck Band, ch 1, sc in end of same row and in end of each of next 21 rows, turn. *(22 sc)*

Rows 2–4: Ch 1, sc in each st across, turn.

Row 5: Ch 1, 2 sc in first st, sc in each st across to last st with 2 sc in last st, turn. *(24 sc)*

Row 6: Ch 1, sc in each st across, turn.

Rows 7–19: Rep rows 5 and 6 alternately, ending with row 5 and *(38 sts)*. Fasten off.

Border
Row 1: With RS facing, working around 3 edges of Collar, join royal blue with sl st in end of next unworked row on Neck Band, sc in end of row 1 of Collar, sc in end of each row across to corner, 3 sc in corner st, sc in each st across row 19 to next corner, 3 sc in corner st, sc in end st of each row across to Neck Band, sl st in end of next unworked row on Neck Band. Fasten off.

Row 2: With RS facing, join white with sl st in end st of next unworked row on Neck Band after first sl st of row 1 of Border, sc in first sc of row 1 of Border and in each sc across, working 3 sc in each corner sc, ending with sl st in next unworked row on Neck Band. Fasten off.

With sewing needle and thread, sew 1 button to each bottom corner of Collar.

Bow
Row 1: With red, ch 2, sc in 2nd ch from hook, turn. *(1 sc)*

Row 2: Ch 1, 2 sc in sc, turn. *(2 sc)*

Row 3: Ch 1, 2 sc in each of 2 sc, turn. *(4 sc)*

Rows 4–37: Ch 1, sc in each st across, turn.

Row 38: Ch 1, sc dec in first 2 sts, sc dec in last 2 sts, turn. *(2 sts)*

Row 39: Sc dec in last 2 sts. Fasten off. Tie loose overhand knot at center of Bow to form knot with 2 ends hanging. With tapestry needle and red, sew Bow to end of Neck Band. ❏❏

Flower Garden Bolero

Design by Sue Childress

FINISHED SIZES

Fits woman's bust size 30 to 32-inch (small) [34 to 36 inch (medium), 38 to 49 inch (large)] Pattern is written for smallest size with changes for larger sizes in brackets.

FINISHED GARMENT MEASUREMENT

Chest: 40 [48, 56] inches
Length: 24 [28, 32] inches

MATERIALS

❑ Medium (worsted) weight yarn (2.5 oz/121 yds/50g per skein): 3 [4, 5] skeins MC 1 [2, 2] each of 6 assorted CCs
❑ Size F/5/3.75mm crochet hook or size needed to obtain gauge
❑ Sewing needle
❑ Sewing thread
❑ 4 [5, 5] ⅞-inch buttons

GAUGE

Motif = 3½ inches between opposite points.
Take time to check your gauge.

INSTRUCTIONS
MOTIF

Rnd 1 (RS): With any CC, ch 6, sl st in first ch to form ring, ch 1, 12 sc in ring, join with sl st in beg sc. *(12 sc)*

Rnd 2: Ch 1, sc in first st, ch 6, [sk next sc, sc in next sc, ch 6] 5 times, sk last sc, join with sl st in beg sc. *(6 ch, 6 sps)*

Rnd 3: Ch 1, sc in first st, 10 hdc in next ch-6 sp, [sc in next sc, 10 hdc in next ch-6 sp] 5 times, join with sl st in beg sc. Fasten off.

Make a total of 56 [80, 106] motifs in desired CCs.

JOINING MOTIFS IN ROWS

Motif Row 1: With RS facing, using joining diagram as guide, join MC with sl st between 5th and 6th hdc on any petal of any Motif, working across top half of Motif, ch 1, 2 sc in same sp, *[ch 5, 2 sc in next sc on same Motif, ch 5, 2 sc between 5th and 6th hdc on next petal of same Motif] 3 times**, with RS facing, working across top half of next Motif, 2 sc between 5th and 6th hdc of any petal on next Motif, rep from * across until last Motif for size being worked has been joined, ending last rep at **, working across opposite half of each Motif on row, [ch 5, 2 sc in next sc on same Motif, ch 5, 2 sc between 5th and 6th hdc on next petal of same Motif] twice, ch 5, 2 sc in next sc on same Motif, ◊ch 5, 2 sc over joined sts between Motifs, ch 5, 2 sc in next sc on next Motif, [ch 5, 2 sc between 5th and 6th hdc on same Motif, ch 5, 2 sc in next sc on same Motif] twice, rep from ◊ across, ending with ch 5, join with sl st in beg sc. Fasten off.

Motif Rows 2–6 [2–7, 2–8]: Rep Motif Row 1, joining as many Motifs as is indicated on joining diagram for desired size.

Rows 5 & 6 [5 & 7, 6 & 8] will each have 3 separate sections to divide for right front, back and left front.

JOINING ROWS

Rows 1 & 2: With RS facing, beg at right-hand edge, join MC with sl st in ch-5 sp on first Motif of row 2 at point A indicated on Diagram A, ch 1, 2 sc in same ch sp, ch 2, 2 sc in next ch-5 sp on first Motif of row 1 at point B indicated on Diagram A, continue across, following Diagram A, until all Motifs on row 2 have be joined to row 1. Fasten off.
Continuing in established pattern, join rem rows.

Shoulder Seams

Matching points indicated on joining diagram, join shoulder seams in established pattern for Joining Rows.

Vest Edging

With RS facing, join MC with sl st in any ch-5 sp at center back neck opening, ch 1, beg in same ch sp, 6 sc in same ch and in each ch-5 sp around with 2 sc in each ch-2 sp around entire outer edge of vest, join with sl st in beg sc. Fasten off.

Armhole Edging

With RS facing join MC with sl st in any ch-5 sp on either armhole, ch 1, beg in same ch sp, 6 sc in the same ch and in each ch-5 sp around with 2 sc in each ch-2 sp around, join with sl st in beg sc. Fasten off.
Rep on rem armhole.

Buttonhole Band

With RS facing, join MC with sl st in 3rd sc of 6-sc group over ch-5 sp at bottom of right front opening at point indicated on Diagram A, ch 1, sc in same st and in each of next 8 sc, [ch 5, sk next sc, sc in each of next 25 sc] 3 [4, 4] times, ch 5, sk next sc, sc in each of next 12 sc, sl st in next st. Fasten off.

Finishing

Sew buttons on left front opening opposite buttonholes.
Using joining diagram as guide, fold 1 Motif at top corner of each front opening in half to WS, tack in place with sewing thread. ❑❑

Diagram A

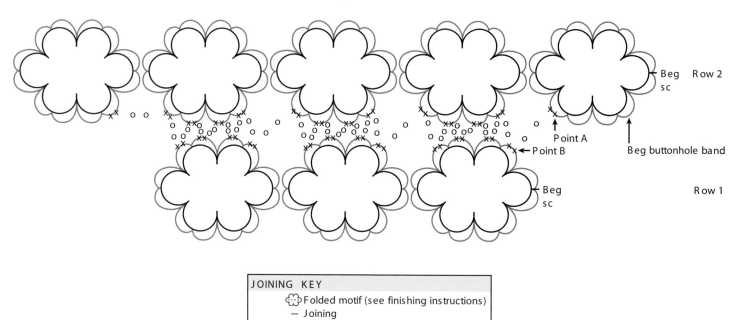

Beg Row 2
sc

Point A
Point B

Beg buttonhole band

Beg Row 1
sc

Large Joining Diagram

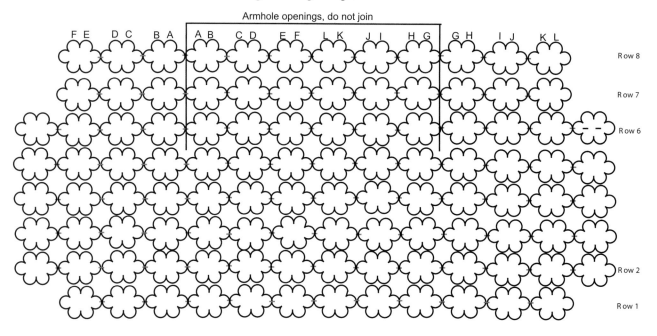

Armhole openings, do not join

F E   D C   B A   A B   C D   E F   L K   J I   H G   G H   I J   K L

Row 8
Row 7
Row 6
Row 2
Row 1

Medium Joining Diagram

Armhole openings, do not join

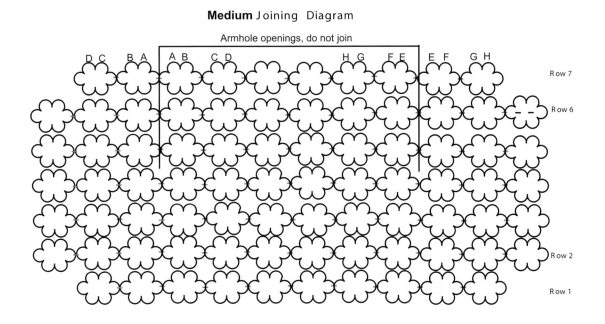

D C   B A   A B   C D   H G   F E   E F   G H   Row 7

Row 6

Row 2

Row 1

Small Joining Diagram

Armhole openings, do not join

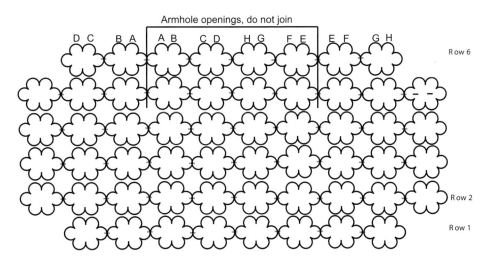

D C   B A   A B   C D   H G   F E   E F   G H   Row 6

Row 2

Row 1

Ponytail Pretties

Designs by Lori Zeller

SKILL LEVEL
■□□□
BEGINNER

FINISHED SIZES
2 to 2½ inches in diameter

MATERIALS
❑ Crochet cotton size 10:
  Small amounts shaded
  purples, pastels ombré,
  raspberry, delft blue
  and white
❑ Size 5/1.90mm steel crochet
  hook or size needed to
  obtain gauge
❑ Tapestry needle
❑ 5 each light pink and light
  blue pony beads
❑ 5 rubber hair bands

GAUGE
11 dc = 1 inch

SPECIAL STITCHES
  V-stitch (V-st): (Dc, ch 1, dc) in
  indicated ch sp.

  Shell: (2 dc, ch 2, 2 dc) in indicated
  ch sp.

INSTRUCTIONS
SHADED PURPLES SCRUNCHIE
Rnd 1 (RS): Join shaded purples with
sl st to hair band, ch 1, [sc around
hair band, ch 3] 51 times, join with
sl st in beg sc. *(53 ch-3 sps)*
Rnd 2: Sl st into ch-3 sp, ch 4 *(counts
as first dc and ch 1)*, dc in same ch-3
sp *(beg V-st)*, **V-st** *(see Special Stitches)*
in each ch-3 sp around, join with sl
st in 3rd ch of beg ch-4.
Rnd 3: Sl st into ch-1 sp of V-st, ch 1, (sc,
ch 2, dc) in same ch-1 sp of V-st, (sc, ch
2, dc) in ch-1 sp of each V-st around,
join with sl st in beg sc. Fasten off.

PASTELS OMBRÉ SCRUNCHIE
Rnd 1 (RS): Join pastels ombré with
sl st to hair band, ch 3 *(counts as first
dc throughout)*, work 59 dc around
hair band, join with sl st in 3rd ch
of beg ch-3. *(60 dc)*

Rnd 2: Ch 1, sc in same st as beg ch-1,
ch 3, sk next dc, [sc in next dc, ch
3, sk next dc] around, join with sl st
in beg sc. *(30 ch-3 sps)*
Rnd 3: Sl st into ch-3 sp, ch 1, sc in
same ch-3 sp, ch 1, (dc, ch 1) 4 times
in next ch-3 sp, [sc in next ch-3 sp,
ch 1, (dc, ch 1) 4 times in next ch-3
sp] around, join with sl st in beg sc.
Fasten off.

RASPBERRY SCRUNCHIE
Rnd 1 (RS): Join raspberry with sl st
to hair band, ch 1, [sc around hair
band, ch 3] 45 times, join with sl st
in beg sc. *(45 ch-3 sps)*
Rnd 2: Sl st into ch-3 sp, ch 1, sc in
same ch-3 sp, ch 3, dc in last sc,
[sc in next ch-3 sp, ch 3, dc in last
sc] around, join with sl st in beg sc.
Fasten off.

BEADED SCRUNCHIE
Rnd 1 (RS): String pony beads onto
white cotton alternating bead colors,
join with sl st to hair band, ch 1, [sc
around hair band, ch 3] 50 times, join
with sl st in beg sc. *(50 ch-3 sps)*
Rnd 2: Sl st into ch-3 sp, ch 1, sc in

same ch-3 sp, ch 3, [sc in next ch-3
sp, ch 3] around, join with sl st in
beg sc.
Rnd 3: Sl st into ch-3 sp, ch 1, sc in
same ch-3 sp, ch 1, pull bead up
next to hook, ch 1 over bead, ch 1,
[sc in next ch-3 sp, ch 3] 4 times,
*sc in next ch-3 sp, ch 1, pull bead
up to hook, ch 1 over bead, ch 1,
[sc in next ch-3 sp, ch 3] 4 times,
rep from * around, join with sl st in
beg sc. Fasten off.

DELFT BLUE SCRUNCHIE
Rnd 1 (RS): Join delft blue with sl st to
hair band, ch 1, [sc, ch 3] 52 times
around hair band, join with sl st in
beg sc. *(52 ch-3 sps)*
Rnd 2: Sl st into ch-3 sp, ch 11, sc in
same ch-3 sp, ch 1, **shell** *(see Special
Stitches)* in next ch-3 sp, ch 1, [sc
in next ch-3 sp, ch 1, shell in next
ch-3 sp, ch 1] around, join with sl
st in beg sc.
Rnd 3: Ch 1, sc in first sc, ch 3, (sc, ch
3, sc) in ch-2 sp of shell, ch 3, [sc in
next sc, ch 3, (sc, ch 3, sc) in next
ch-2 sp of shell, ch 3] around, join
with sl st in beg sc. Fasten off. ❑❑

Rainbow Set

Designs by Tammy Hildebrand

FINISHED SIZES
Scarf: 5½ x 51½ inches
Beret: One size fits most

MATERIALS
❑ Medium (worsted) weight yarn:
  8 oz/400 yds/227g black
  2 oz/100 yds/57g each 5
  assorted colors
❑ Size J/10/6mm crochet hook or
  size needed to obtain gauge

GAUGE
Scarf: 3 dc = 1 inch, 6 pattern rows =
3 inches
Beret: Rnds 1–3 = 3½ inches across

PATTERN NOTE
Do not turn at end of rows, unless
otherwise stated.

INSTRUCTIONS
SCARF
Row 1: With black, ch 19, dc in 4th ch
(first 3 chs count as first dc) from hook
and in each ch across, **do not turn**
(see Pattern Note). Fasten off. *(17 dc)*
Row 2: Join color with sc in first st,
***fpdc** (see Stitch Guide),* around post
of next st, sc in next st, rep from *
across. Fasten off.
Row 3: Join black with sl st in first st,
ch 3 *(counts as first dc)*, dc in each
st across. Fasten off.
Row 4: Join color with sc in first st,
[fpdc around next st, sc in next st]
across. Fasten off.
Rows 5–103: Rep rows 3 and 4 alternately, ending with row 3.

Fringe
For each fringe, cut 2 (8-inch) lengths.
Fold all strands in half, insert hook
in st, pull fold through st, pull ends
through fold, tighten. Trim ends.
Alternating black and colors, fringe in
each st across each short edge.

HAT

Rnd 1: With black, ch 4, sl st in first ch to form ring, ch 3, 21 dc in ring, join with sl st in 3rd ch of beg ch-3. Fasten off. *(22 dc)*

Rnd 2: Join color with sc in first st, fpdc around next st, [sc in next st, fpdc around next st] around, join with sl st in beg sc. Fasten off.

Rnd 3: Join black with sl st in first st, (ch 3, dc) in same st, dc in next st, [2 dc in next st, dc in next st] around, join with sl st in 3rd ch of beg ch-3. Fasten off. *(33 dc)*

Rnd 4: Join color with sc in first st, sc in next st, fpdc around next st, [sc in each of next 2 sts, fpdc around next st] around, join with last in first sc. Fasten off.

Rnd 5: Join black with sl st in first st, ch 3, dc in next st, 2 dc in next st, [dc in each of next 2 sts, 2 dc in next st] around, join with sl st in 3rd ch of beg ch-3. Fasten off. *(44 dc)*

Rnd 6: Join color with sc in first st, fpdc around next st, [sc in next st, fpdc around next st] around, join with sl st in beg sc. Fasten off.

Rnd 7: Join black with sl st in first st, (ch 3, dc) in same st, dc in next st, [2 dc in next st, dc in next st] around, join with sl st in 3rd ch of beg ch-3. Fasten off. *(66 dc)*

Rnd 8: Join color with sc in first st, fpdc around next st, [sc in next st, fpdc around next st] around, join with sl st in beg sc. Fasten off.

Rnd 9: Join black with sl st in first st, ch 3, dc in next st, [2 dc in next st, dc in next st] around, join with sl st in 3rd ch of beg ch-3. Fasten off. *(98 dc)*

Rnd 10: Join color with sc in first st, fpdc around next st, [sc in next st, fpdc around next st] around, join with sl st in beg sc. Fasten off.

Rnd 11: Join black with sl st in first st, ch 3, dc in each st around, join with sl st in 3rd ch of beg ch-3. Fasten off.

Rnd 12: Join color with sc in first st, fpdc around next st, [sc in next st, fpdc around next st] around, join with sl st in beg sc. Fasten off.

Rnd 13: Join black with sl st in first st, ch 3, dc in next st, [**dc dec** *(see Stitch Guide)* in next 2 sts, dc in next st] around, join with sl st in 3rd ch of beg ch-3. Fasten off. *(66 dc)*

Rnd 14: Join color with sc in first st, fpdc around next st, [sc in next st, fpdc around next st] around, join with sl st in beg sc. Fasten off.

Rnd 15: Join black with sl st in first st, ch 3, dc dec in next 2 sts, [dc in next st, dc dec in next 2 sts] around, join with sl st in 3rd ch of beg ch-3. Fasten off. *(44 dc)*

Rnd 16: Join color with sc in first st, fpdc around next st, [sc in next st, fpdc around next st] around, join with sl st in beg sc. Fasten off.

Rnd 17: Join black with sc in first st, sc in each st around, join with sl st in beg sc.

Rnds 18–22: Ch 1, sc in each st around, join with sl st in top of beg sc. At end of last rnd, fasten off. ❑❑

Lacy Tissue Cover

Design by Michele Wilcox

SKILL LEVEL
■■□□□
BEGINNER

FINISHED SIZE
Fits standard boutique-style tissue box

MATERIALS
- ❑ Medium (worsted) weight yarn:
  3½ oz/175 yds/99g blue
  ½ oz/25 yds/14g white
  Small amount light pink
- ❑ Size 3 pearl cotton:
  Small amount each green, dark pink and yellow
- ❑ Size F/5/3.75 crochet hook or size needed to obtain gauge
- ❑ Stitch markers
- ❑ Tapestry needle
- ❑ Embroidery needle
- ❑ 1 yd pink ¼-inch satin ribbon

GAUGE
9 sc = 2 inches, 9 sc rows = 2 inches

INSTRUCTIONS

TISSUE COVER

Side

Make 4.

Row 1 (WS): With blue, ch 19, sc in 2nd ch from hook and in each ch across, turn. *(18 sc)*

Rows 2–25: Ch 1, sc in each st across, turn. At end of last row, fasten off.

Top

Row 1: With blue, ch 19, sc in 2nd ch from hook, and in each ch across, turn. *(18 sc)*

Rows 2–9: Ch 1, sc in each st across, turn.

Row 10: Ch 1, sc in each of first 4 sts, for **opening**, ch 10, sk next 10 sts, sc in each of last 4 sts, turn.

Row 11: Ch 1, sc in each sc and in each ch across, turn.

Rows 12–18: Ch 1, sc in each st across, turn. At end of last row, fasten off.

Assembly

Matching sts, with blue, sc Sides and Top tog forming box.

Trim

Join white with sc in any st, [ch 3, sc in next st] around bottom, Sides and Top as shown in photo.

HEART

Row 1: With light pink, ch 2, 3 sc in 2nd ch from hook, turn. *(3 sc)*

Row 2: Ch 1, 2 sc in first st, sc in each st across with 2 sc in last st, turn. *(5 sc)*

Row 3: Ch 1, sc in each st across, turn.

Rows 4–5: Ch 1, 2 sc in first st, sc in each st across with 2 sc in last st, turn. *(7 sc, 9 sc)*

Row 6: Ch 1, sc in each st across, turn.

Row 7: Ch 1, 2 sc in first st, sc in each st across with 2 sc in last st, turn. *(11 sc)*

Rows 8–9: Ch 1, sc in each st across, turn.

Row 10: For **first side**, ch 1, sc in each of first 5 sts leaving rem sts unworked, turn. *(5 sc)*

Row 11: Ch 1, **sc dec** *(see Stitch Guide)* in first 2 sts, sc in next st, sc dec in last 2 sts, turn. Fasten off. *(3 sc)*

Row 10: For **2nd side**, sk next st on row 9, join light pink with sc in next st, sc in each of last 4 sts, turn. *(5 sc)*

Row 11: Ch 1, sc dec in first 2 sts, sc in next st, sc dec in last 2 sts, **do not turn.**

Rnd 12: Working around outer edge, ch 1, sc in each st and in end of each row around with 2 sc in upper corners and 3 sc in tip of heart, join with sl st in first sc. Fasten off. *(34 sc)*

Trim

Join white with sl st in center top st of Heart, (sc, hdc, ch 2, hdc, sc) in next st, *sl st in next st, (sc, hdc, ch 2, hdc, sc) in next st, rep from * around, join with sl st in first sl st. Fasten off.

With dark pink and yellow, using French Knot *(see illustration)*, embroider flowers according to illustration.

French Knot

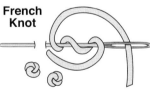

With green, using Straight and Lazy Daisy Stitches *(see illustrations)*, embroider leaves and stems according to illustration. Sew Heart to 1 Side of box.

Straight Stitch

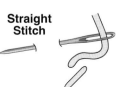

Lazy Daisy Stitch

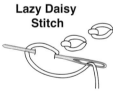

Starting in corner above Heart, weave ribbon through ch sps around top of Cover, tie into a bow on corner. ❏❏

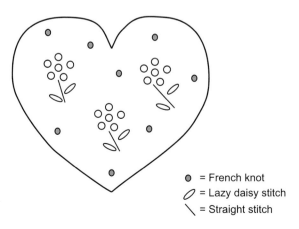

● = French knot
⬭ = Lazy daisy stitch
╲ = Straight stitch

Wild With Color

Design by Patricia Hall

FINISHED SIZE
44½ x 77½ inches

MATERIALS
- ❏ Medium (worsted) weight yarn:
  20 oz/1,000 yds/567g black
  Assorted colors for 9 Panels:
  1½ oz/75 yds/43g each of
  A, B and C for each Panel
  1 oz/ 50 yds/28g each of
  yellow and green
- ❏ Size H/8/5mm crochet hook or
  size needed to obtain gauge

GAUGE
7 sts and chs = 2 inches, rnd 5 =
4 inches across

SPECIAL STITCH
Popcorn (pc): 5 dc in center dc
of next 3-dc group on rnd before
last, drop lp from hook, insert hook
through first dc of group, place lp
on hook, pull through st.

INSTRUCTIONS
AFGHAN
Panel
Make 9.

Row 1: With yellow, ch 241, dc in 5th
ch from hook, dc in each of next 2
chs, [ch 1, sk next ch, dc in each of
next 3 chs] across to last 2 chs, ch
4, sk next st, sl st in last st. Fasten
off. *(59 dc groups, 58 ch-1 sp, 2 ch-4
sps at ends)*

Rnd 2: Join A with sl st in last ch-1
sp made, ch 3 *(counts as first dc)*,
dc in same ch sp, ch 1, (3 dc, ch 1)
4 times in end ch-4 sp, working
across starting ch on opposite side
of row 1, [3 dc in next ch-1 sp, ch 1]
across to ch-4 sp at other end, (3 dc,
ch 1) 4 times in end ch-4 sp, [3 dc
in next ch-1 sp, ch 1] across, dc in
same ch-1 sp as beg ch-3, join with
sl st in top of beg ch-3. Fasten off.
(124 ch-1 sps)

Rnd 3: Join B with sl st in last ch-1 sp
made, ch 3, dc in same ch sp, ch 1,
3 dc in next ch-1 sp, ch 1, *(3 dc, ch
1) twice in next ch-1 sp, 3 dc in next
ch-1 sp, ch 1, (3 dc, ch 1) twice in
next ch-1 sp, 3 dc in next ch-1 sp,
ch 1, (3 dc, ch 1) twice in next ch-1
sp*, [3 dc in next ch-1 sp, ch 1] 59
times, rep between *, [3 dc in next
ch-1 sp, ch 1] across, dc in same ch-1
sp as beg ch-3, join with sl st in beg
ch-3. Fasten off. *(128 ch-1 sps)*

Rnd 4: Join C with sl st in last ch-1 sp
made, ch 3, dc in same ch sp, ch 1,
[3 dc in next ch-1 sp, ch 1] twice,
*(3 dc, ch 1) twice in next corner
ch-1 sp, [3 dc in next ch-1 sp, ch
1] twice, (3 dc, ch 1) twice in next
corner ch-1 sp*, [3 dc in next ch-1
sp, ch 1] 60 times, rep between *,
[3 dc in next ch-1 sp, ch 1] across,
dc in same ch-1 sp as beg ch-3, join
with sl st in top of beg ch-3. Fasten
off. *(132 ch-1 sps)*

Rnd 5: Join black with sc in first dc of
first 3-dc group worked in first corner
ch sp, ch 2, [sc in next dc, ch 2] twice,
complete rnd as follows:

A. (Sc, ch 3, sc) in corner ch-1 sp, (ch
2, sc) in each of next 3 dc, ***pc** *(see
Special Stitches)*, sk next ch-1 sp on
last rnd, sc in next dc, [ch 2, sc in
next dc] twice, rep from * twice, (sc,
ch 3, sc) in corner ch-1 sp;

B. (Ch 2, sc) in each of next 3 dc;

C. [Dc in center dc of next 3-dc group
on rnd before last, sk next ch-1 sp
on last rnd, sc in each of next 3 dc]
60 times, dc in center dc of next
3-dc group on rnd before last, sk
next ch-1 sp on last rnd;

D. (Sc, ch 2) in each of next 3 dc;

E. Rep steps A and B;

F. Dc in center dc of next 3-dc group
on rnd before last, sk next ch-1 sp
on last rnd, [sc in each of next 3 dc,
dc in center dc of next 3-dc group
on rnd before last, sk next ch-1 sp
on last rnd] across, join with sl st in
beg sc. Fasten off. *(61 dc, 60 3-sc
groups on each long edge)*

Rnd 6: Join green with sc in center dc
of last 3-dc group on rnd 1, ch 2, sc
in each of next 3 dc on rnd 2, *[ch
2, sc in next ch-4 sp on rnd 1, ch 2,
sc in each of next 3 dc on rnd 2] 3
times*, [ch 2, sc in center dc of next
3-dc group on rnd 1, ch 2, sc in next
each of next 3 dc on rnd 2] across
to ch-4 sp at other end, rep between
*, [ch 2, sc in center dc of next 3-dc
group on rnd 1, ch 2, sc in each of
next 3 dc on rnd 2] across, ch 2, join
with sl st in beg sc. Fasten off.

Assembly
Hold 2 Panels side-by-side with RS
up, matching dc and 3-sc groups,
join black with sc in first dc at right,
ch 2, sc in first dc at left, working
in sc and in dc, [ch 2, sc in next st
at right, ch 2, sc in next st at left]
across, ending with last 2 sc worked
in last 2 dc. Fasten off.
Rep until all Panels are joined.

Edging
With RS facing, working along 1 long
edge, join black with sl st in first dc,
[ch 2, sk next st, sl st in next st] across
with last sl st in last sc. Fasten off.
Rep on rem long edge. ❏❏

Repeating Rainbows

Design by Carolyn Pfeifer

SKILL LEVEL

BEGINNER

FINISHED SIZE
40 x 45 inches

MATERIALS
- ❑ Medium (worsted) weight yarn:
  5 oz/250 yds/142g each red,
  orange, yellow, green, blue
  and lavender
- ❑ Size I/9/5.5mm crochet hook
  or size needed to obtain gauge

GAUGE
7 sc = 2 inches, 7 rows =
2 inches

INSTRUCTIONS

AFGHAN
Row 1: With red, ch 143, sc in 2nd ch from hook and in each ch across, turn. *(142 sc)*

Row 2: Ch 1, sc in each st across, turn. Fasten off.

Row 3: Join orange with sc in first st, sc in each st across, turn.

Row 4: Ch 1, sc in each st across, turn. Fasten off.

Row 5: Join yellow with sc in first st, sc in each st across, turn.

Row 6: Ch 1, sc in each st across, turn. Fasten off.

Row 7: Join green with sc in first st, sc in each st across, turn.

Row 8: Ch 1, sc in each st across, turn. Fasten off.

Row 9: Join blue with sc in first st, sc in each st across, turn.

Row 10: Ch 1, sc in each st across, turn. Fasten off.

Row 11: Join lavender with sc in first st, sc in each st across, turn.

Row 12: Ch 1, sc in each st across, turn. Fasten off.

Row 13: Join red with sc in first st, sc in each of next 3 sts, [ch 3, sk next 2 sts, sc in next st] 44 times, ch 3, sk next 2 sts, sc in each of last 4 sts, turn. *(45 ch-3 sps)*

Row 14: Ch 1, working in **front lps** *(see Stitch Guide)*, sc in each of first 4 sts, 3 sc in next ch sp, sc in next ch sp, [5 sc in next ch sp, sc in next ch sp] across with 4 sc in last ch sp, sc in front lp in each of last 4 sts, turn. Fasten off. *(142 sc)*

Row 15: Join orange with sc in first st, sc in each of next 3 sts, [ch 3, sk next 2 sts, sc in next st] 44 times, ch 3, sk next 2 sts, sc in each of last 4 sts, turn.

Row 16: Ch 1, working in front lps, sc in each of first 4 sts, 3 sc in next ch sp, sc in next ch sp, [5 sc in next ch sp, sc in next ch sp] across with 4 sc in last ch sp, sc in front lp in each of last 4 sts, turn. Fasten off.

Row 17: Join yellow with sc in first st, sc in each of next 3 sts, [ch 3, sk next 2 sts, sc in next st] 44 times, ch 3, sk next 2 sts, sc in each of last 4 sts, turn.

Row 18: Ch 1, working in front lps, sc in each of first 4 sts, 3 sc in next ch sp, sc in next ch sp, [5 sc in next ch sp, sc in next ch sp] across with 4 sc in last ch sp, sc in front lp in each of last 4 sts, turn. Fasten off.

Row 19: Join green with sc in first st, sc in each of next 3 sts, [ch 3, sk next 2 sts, sc in next st] 44 times, ch 3, sk next 2 sts, sc in each of last 4 sts, turn.

Row 20: Ch 1, working in front lps, sc in each of first 4 sts, 3 sc in next ch sp, sc in next ch sp, [5 sc in next ch sp, sc in next ch sp] across with 4 sc in last ch sp, sc in front lp in each of last 4 sts, turn. Fasten off.

Row 21: Join blue with sc in first st, sc in each of next 3 sts, [ch 3, sk next 2 sts, sc in next st] 44 times, ch 3, sk next 2 sts, sc in each of last 4 sts, turn.

Row 22: Ch 1, working in front lps, sc in each of first 4 sts, 3 sc in next ch sp, sc in next ch sp, [5 sc in next ch sp, sc in next ch sp] across with 4 sc in last ch sp, sc in front lp in each of last 4 sts, turn. Fasten off.

Row 23: Join lavender with sc in first st, sc in each of next 3 sts, [ch 3, sk next 2 sts, sc in next st] 44 times, ch 3, sk next 2 sts, sc in each of last 4 sts, turn.

Row 24: Ch 1, working in front lps, sc in each of first 4 sts, 3 sc in next ch sp, sc in next ch sp, [5 sc in next ch sp, sc in next ch sp] across with 4 sc in last ch sp, sc in front lp in each of last 4 sts, turn. Fasten off.

Row 25: Join red with sc in first st, sc in each st across, turn.

Rows 26–156: Rep rows 2–25 consecutively, ending with row 12. At end of last row, fasten off.

Fringe
Cut 2 strands 8 inches in length, holding both strands tog, fold in half, pull fold through st, pull ends through fold. Pull to tighten.

Matching colors, fringe in every other st across short ends of Afghan. ❑❑

Color Wheels

Designs by Tammy Hildebrand

SKILL LEVEL

■ ■ ■ ☐

INTERMEDIATE

FINISHED SIZES
Afghan: 44 x 64 inches
Pillow: 16 inches in diameter, not including Edging

MATERIALS
❑ Red Heart Super Saver medium (worsted) weight yarn:
   25 oz/1250 yds/709g #316 soft white
   5 oz/250 yds/142g each #886 blue, #358 lavender, #774 light raspberry, #356 amethyst, #885 delft blue, #324 bright yellow and #319 cherry red
❑ Red Heart Classic medium (worsted) weight yarn:
   5 oz/250 yds/42g #48 teal
❑ Size I/9/5.5mm crochet hook or size needed to obtain gauge
❑ Tapestry needle
❑ 16-inch round pillow form or fiberfill

GAUGE
Rnds 1 and 2 = 2¼ inches in diameter

PATTERN NOTES
Wind 2 (10-yard) balls of each color except soft white for each Motif.

Wind 2 (12-yard) balls of each color except soft white for Pillow.

Change color (see Stitch Guide) in last stitch made.

Use each color then repeat sequence. Maintain color sequence in each round.

INSTRUCTIONS
AFGHAN
Motif
Make 12.
Rnd 1: With soft white, ch 3, sl st in first ch to form ring, ch 1, 16 sc in ring, join with sl st in beg sc. Fasten off. (16 sc)

Rnd 2: Join color with sl st in any st, ch 3 (counts as first dc throughout), dc in same st changing to next color, [2 dc in next st changing to next color] 15 times, join with sl st in 3rd ch of beg ch-3. (32 dc)

Rnd 3: Ch 3, dc in next st changing to next color, [dc in each of next 2 sts changing to next color] around, join with sl st in 3rd ch of beg ch 3.

Rnd 4: Ch 3, dc in same st, dc in next st changing to next color, [2 dc in next st, dc in next st changing to next color] around, join with sl st in 3rd ch of beg ch-3. (48 dc)

Rnd 5: Ch 3, dc in each of next 2 sts changing to next color, [dc in each of next 3 sts changing to next color] around, join with sl st in 3rd ch of beg ch-3.

Rnd 6: Ch 3, dc in same st, dc in each of next 2 sts changing to next color, [2 dc in next st, dc in each of next 2 sts changing to next color] around, join with sl st in 3rd ch of beg ch-3. (64 dc)

Rnd 7: Ch 3, dc in each of next 3 sts changing to next color, [dc in each of next 4 sts changing to next color] around, join with sl st in 3rd ch of beg ch 3

Rnd 8: Ch 3, dc in same st, dc in each of next 3 sts changing to next color, [2 dc in next st, dc in each of next 3 sts changing to next color] around, join with sl st in 3rd ch of beg ch-3. Fasten off all colors. (80 dc)

Rnd 9: Join soft white with sc in sp between colors, 2 sc in same sp, *sk next 2 sts, 3 sc in next st, (2 dc, ch 2, 2 dc) in sp between colors, sk next 2 sts, 3 sc in next st**, 3 sc in next sp between colors, rep from * around, ending last rep at **, join with sl st in beg sc.

Rnd 10: Ch 3, dc in each of next 5 sts, *(2 dc, ch 2, 2 dc) in next ch-2 sp, sk next 2 sts**, dc in each of next 9 sts, rep from * around, ending last rep at **, dc in each of last 3 sts, join with sl st in 3rd ch of beg ch-3. Fasten off.

Rnd 11: Join any color with sc in any ch-2 sp, 4 sc in same ch sp, *[ch 1, sk next st, sc in next st] 6 times, ch 1**, 5 sc in next ch-2 sp, rep from * around, ending last rep at **, join with sl st in beg sc. Fasten off.

Rnd 12: Working this rnd in **back lps** (see Stitch Guide), join soft white with sl st in first st of any corner group, ch 2 (counts as first hdc), sk next st, *(sc, ch 2, sc) in next st, sk next st, hdc in next st, dc in each of next 13 sts or chs**, hdc in next st, sk next st, rep from * around, ending last rep at **, join with sl st in 2nd ch of beg ch-2. Fasten off.

Sew Motifs tog according to illustration.

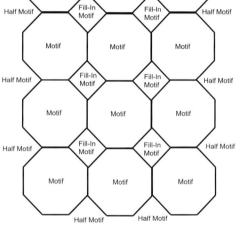

Join Edging here.

Half Motif · Half Motif · Motif · Motif · Motif · Half Motif · Fill-In Motif · Fill-In Motif · Half Motif · Motif · Motif · Motif · Half Motif · Fill-In Motif · Fill-In Motif · Half Motif · Motif · Motif · Motif · Half Motif · Fill-In Motif · Fill-In Motif · Half Motif · Motif · Motif · Motif · Half Motif · Half Motif

Fill-In Motif
Make 6.
Rnd 1: With soft white, ch 4, sl st in first ch to form ring, ch 3, 15 dc in ring, join with sl st in 3rd ch of beg ch-3. Fasten off. (16 dc)

Rnd 2: Join any color with sl st in any st, ch 3, dc in same st changing to next color, [2 dc in next st changing to next color] around, join with sl st in 3rd ch of beg ch-3. Fasten off all colors.

Rnd 3: Join soft white with sl st in sp between colors, ch 5 (counts as first dc and ch-2), dc in same sp, *3 sc in next sp between colors, sc in next sp between colors, 3 sc in next sp

between colors**, (dc, ch 2, dc) in next sp between colors, rep from * around, ending last rep at **, join with sl st in 3rd ch of beg ch-5.

Rnd 4: Sl st in ch sp, ch 3, (dc, ch 2, 2 dc) in same ch sp, *sk next st, dc in each of next 7 sts**, (2 dc, ch 2, 2 dc) in next ch-2 sp, rep from * around, ending last rep at **, join with sl st in 3rd ch of beg ch-3. Fasten off.

Rnd 5: Join color with sc in any ch-2 sp, 4 sc in same ch sp, ch 1, sk next st, [sc in next st, ch 1, sk next st] 5 times**, 5 sc in next ch-2 sp, rep from * around, ending last rep at **, join with sl st in beg sc. Fasten off.

Rnd 6: Working in back lps, join soft white with sl st in first st of any 5 sc group, ch 3, sk next st, *(2 dc, ch 2, 2 dc) in next st, sk next st**, dc in each of next 13 sts and chs, sk next st, rep from * around, ending last rep at **, dc in each st and in each ch around, join with sl st in beg sc. Fasten off.

Sew back lps of Motifs in openings between Motifs according to illustration.

Half Motif
Make 10.
Row 1: With soft white, ch 3, sl st in first ch to form ring, ch 3, 7 dc in ring, **do not turn.** Fasten off. *(8 dc)*

Row 2: Join color with sl st in first st, ch 3 dc in same st changing to next color, [2 dc in next st changing to next color] across, do not change color in last st. Fasten off all colors. *(16 dc)*

Row 3: Join soft white with sl st in first st, ch 3, dc in same st, 3 sc in next sp between colors, sc in next sp between colors, 3 sc in next sp between colors, (2 dc, ch 2, 2 dc) in next sp between colors, 3 sc in next sp between colors, sc in next sp between colors, 3 sc in next sp between next colors, dc in last st, turn.

Row 4: Ch 3, dc in next 10 sts, (2 dc, ch 2, 2 dc) in next ch-2 sp, dc in each st across, turn. Fasten off.

Row 5: Join color with sc in first st, ch 1, [sc in next st, ch 1, sk next st] across to ch sp, 5 sc in ch-2 sp, [ch 1, sk next st, sc in next st] across with ch 1, sc in last st, **do not turn.** Fasten off.

Row 6: Working in back lps, join soft white with sl st in first st, ch 3, dc in

each st and ch across to next ch-2 sp, (dc, ch 2, dc) in next ch-2 sp, dc in each ch and st across. Fasten off.

Row 7: Working across bottom edge, join soft white with sc in end of row 2, sc in same row, hdc in end of row 1, 3 dc in bottom of ring, hdc in end of row 1, 2 sc in end of row 2. Fasten off.

Sew back lps of Half Motifs to Motifs according to illustration.

Border
Join soft white with sl st in ch-2 sp at top right, ch 5, dc in same ch sp, *[dc in each st across to next ch-2 sp, dc in ch-2 sp, dc in center of joining, working in ends of rows on Half Motif, dc in next row, sk next row, 2 hdc in next row, sc in next row, sc in each of next 9 sts, sc in next row, 2 hdc in next row, sk next row, dc in next row, dc in center of joining, dc in next ch-2 sp] twice, ◊dc in each st across to next ch-2 sp, (dc, ch 2, dc) in next ch-2 sp◊ twice, rep between [ ] 3 times* rep between ◊ twice, rep between *, rep between ◊, dc in each st around, join with sl st in 3rd ch of beg ch-3. Fasten off.

PILLOW
Side
Make 2.
Rnd 1: With soft white, ch 3, sl st in first ch to form ring, ch 1, 16 sc in ring, join with sl st in beg sc. Fasten off. *(16 sc)*

Rnd 2: Join color with sl st in any st, ch 3 *(counts as first dc throughout)*, dc in same st changing to next color, [2 dc in next st changing to next color] 15 times, join with sl st in 3rd ch of beg ch-3. *(32 dc)*

Rnd 3: Ch 3, dc in next st changing to next color, [dc in each of next 2 sts changing to next color] around, join with sl st in 3rd ch of beg ch 3.

Rnd 4: Ch 3, dc in same st, dc in next st changing to next color, [2 dc in next st, dc in next st changing to next color] around, join with sl st in 3rd ch of beg ch-3. *(48 dc)*

Rnd 5: Ch 3, dc in each of next 2 sts changing to next color, [dc in each of next 3 sts changing to next color] around, join with sl st in 3rd ch of beg ch-3.

Rnd 6: Ch 3, dc in same st, dc in each of next 2 sts changing to next color, [2 dc in next st, dc in each of next 2 sts changing to next color] around, join with sl st in 3rd ch of beg ch-3. *(64 dc)*

Rnd 7: Ch 3, dc in each of next 3 sts changing to next color, [dc in each of next 4 sts changing to next color] around, join with sl st in 3rd ch of beg ch-3

Rnd 8: Ch 3, dc in same st, dc in each of next 3 sts changing to next color, [2 dc in next st, dc in each of next 3 sts changing to next color] around, join with sl st in 3rd ch of beg ch-3. *(80 dc)*

Rnd 9: Ch 3, dc in each of next 4 sts changing to next color, [dc in each of next 5 sts changing to next color] around, join with sl st in 3rd ch of beg ch-3.

Rnd 10: Ch 3, dc in same st, dc in each of next 4 sts changing to next color, [2 dc in next st, dc in each of next 4 sts changing to next color] around, join with sl st in 3rd ch of beg ch-3. *(96 dc)*

Rnd 11: Ch 3, dc in each of next 5 sts changing to next color, [dc in each of next 6 sts changing to next color] around, join with sl st in 3rd ch of beg ch-3.

Rnd 12: Ch 3, dc in same st, dc in each of next 5 sts changing to next color, [2 dc in next st, dc in each of next 5 sts changing to next color] around, join with sl st in 3rd ch of beg ch-3. *(112 dc)*

Rnd 13: Ch 3, dc in each of next 6 sts changing to next color, [dc in each of next 7 sts changing to next color] around, join with sl st in 3rd ch of beg ch-3. Fasten off all colors.

Edging
Rnd 1: Holding Side pieces WS tog, working through both thicknesses, join soft white with sc in first st of any color, sc in each st around, inserting pillow form before closing, join with sl st in beg sc.

Rnd 2: Ch 1, sc in first st, sk next 3 sts, 7 dc in next st, [sk next 3 sts, sc in next sp before next st, sk next 3 sts, 7 dc in next st] around, sk last sts, join with sl st in beg sc. Fasten off. ❑❑

Random Acts of Kindness

Design by Michele Thompson

FINISHED SIZE
57 x 59 inches

MATERIALS
- ❑ Medium (worsted) weight yarn:
  68 oz/3,400 yds/1,928g
  assorted colors
- ❑ Size N/15/10mm crochet hook
  or size needed to obtain gauge
- ❑ Tapestry needle

GAUGE
2 strands held tog: 8 dc =
4 inches

PATTERN NOTES
Afghan is worked from side to side.

Use 2 strands held together through-out.

When joining next color and when fastening off previous color at beginnings and ends of rows, leave 3-inch lengths for fringe.

Change color *(see Stitch Guide)* in last stitch made.

INSTRUCTIONS

AFGHAN

Row 1 (RS): With 1 strand each of any 2 colors held tog, ch 122, dc in 4th ch from hook *(first 3 chs count as first dc)* and in each ch across, changing to next 2 colors in last st *(see Pattern Notes)*, turn. Fasten off first 2 colors. *(120 dc)*

Row 2: Ch 3 *(counts as first dc throughout)*, dc in next st and in each st across, changing to next 2 colors in last st, turn. Fasten off previous 2 colors. *(120 dc)*

Next rows: Rep row 2 until afghan measures 57 inches or desired width. At end of last row, fasten off.

Fringe
Tie 3-inch lengths on top and bottom of afghan with square knots for fringe.

Cut 2 (3–inch) lengths of yarn; tie with square knot between first 2 fringe at top. Rep for each sp between fringe across rem of top and across bottom.

Cut 2 (3-inch) lengths of yarn and tie with square knot in first st and in each st across either long edge. Rep for each st across other long edge. ❑❑

Garden Afghan

Design by Dot Drake

SKILL LEVEL

■■■■
EXPERIENCED

FINISHED SIZE
44 x 66 inches

MATERIALS
- ❑ Medium (worsted) weight yarn:
  - 24 oz/1,200 yds/680g aran
  - 12 oz/600 yds/340g
    light mint
  - 6 oz/300 yds/170g each
    pink, lilac, pale plum and
    light coral
- ❑ Size H/8/5mm crochet hook or
  size needed to obtain gauge
- ❑ Tapestry needle

GAUGE
Large motif = 7¼ inches; 2 dc rnds =
1¼ inches

SPECIAL STITCHES
Cluster (cl): [Yo, insert hook in
indicated st, yo, pull up lp, yo, pull
through 2 lps on hook] twice, yo,
pull through all lps on hook.

Shell: (2 dc, ch 3, 2 dc) in top of
ch-5 sp.

INSTRUCTIONS
AFGHAN
Large Motif
Make 54.

Rnd 1: With any color but aran or
light mint, ch 4, dc in 4th ch from
hook, ch 4, [cl (see Special Stitches)
in same ch as beg dc, ch 4] 5 times,
join with sl st in top of first dc. Fasten
off. (6 cls, 6 ch-4 sps)

Rnd 2: Join aran with sl st in any ch-4
sp, ch 3 (counts as first dc throughout),
5 dc in same ch-4 sp, 6 dc in each
ch-4 sp around, join with sl st in 3rd
ch of beg ch-3. (36 dc)

Rnd 3: Join same color yarn as in rnd
1 with sl st in first st, ch 3, dc in each
of next 2 dc, ch 11, remove hook
and drop color to front of Motif,
join light mint in next dc of rnd 2,
ch 3, dc in each of next 2 dc, ch 11,

remove hook and drop light mint to
front of motif, [pick up dropped lp
of color, dc in each of next 3 dc, ch
11, remove hook and drop color to
front of motif, pick up dropped lp
of mint green, dc in each of next 3
dc, ch 11, remove hook and drop
light mint to front of Motif] 5 times,
joining last ch of color to 3rd ch of
beg ch-3 at back of Motif, remove
hook and join light mint at back of
Motif behind color ch-11 sp, join
with sl st in 3rd ch of beg ch-3, **do
not fasten off.** (36 dc, 6 ch-11 lps
each color)

Rnd 4: At back of motif, pick up color,
ch 3, dc in each of next 2 dc, ch 5,
(sc, ch 3, sc) in next color ch-11
sp, ch 5, drop lp of color to back of
motif, pick up mint green lp, ch 3,
dc in each of next 2 dc, ch 5, (sc,
ch 3, sc) in next light mint ch-11 sp,
ch 5, drop lp to back of motif, [pick
up lp of color, at back, dc in each of
next 3 dc, ch 5, (sc, ch 3, sc) in next
color ch-11 sp, ch 5, drop color to
back of motif, pick up light mint at
back of motif, dc in each of next 3
dc, ch 5, (sc, ch 3, sc) in next light
mint ch-11 sp, ch 5, drop lp to back
of work] around, joining each color
and mint green with sl st at back of
motif in 3rd ch of beg ch-3. Fasten
off both yarns.

Note: When working rnd 5, you will
work dc in each of 3 dc of color, shell
in same color ch-5 sp at top. Next, you
will work 3 dc in mint green and shell
in top mint green ch-5 sp.

Rnd 5: Join aran in beg ch-3 of color,
ch 3, dc in each of next 2 dc, **shell**
(see Special Stitches) in top of next
ch-5 sp of color, dc in each of next
3 mint green dc sts, shell in top of
ch-5 mint green sp, [dc in each of
next 3 color dc sts, shell in top of next
ch-5 sp of color, dc in each of next
3 mint green dc sts, shell in top of
next ch-5 sp of mint green] around,
join with sl st in 3rd ch of beg ch-3.
Fasten off.

Continue to make large motifs, joining
into a rectangle of 6 x 9 motifs.

To join motifs, instead of making ch-3
between dc sts of shell on rnd 5, ch
1, sc in adjacent ch-3 sp on previous
motif, ch 1, join 2 consecutive ch-3
sps on each side.

When joining next rows, leave 1 ch-3
sp between each set of joining. There
will be 4 free ch-3 sps in the center
of 4 joined large motifs.

Fill-In Motif
With aran, ch 4, 2 dc in 4th ch from
hook *ch 5, pull lp through first dc
of fill-in motif, 2 sc in ch-5 sp just
made, dc in 2nd of 3-dc group close
to joining of 2 Large Motifs, 3 sc in
ch-5 sp, dc in next 2nd dc of 3-dc
group of next Large Motif, 2 sc in
same ch-5 sp, dc in same first ch of
beg ch-4, ch 1, sc in next ch-3 sp on
Large Motif, ch 1**, 3 dc in same first
ch of beg ch-4, rep from * around,
ending last rep at **, join with sl st in
3rd ch of beg ch-4. Fasten off.

Rep fill-in motif between all joined
Large Motifs.

Edging Motif
Note: Edging motif will be joined between
Large Motifs along all 4 sides of outer
edge of Afghan. Use a different color
for each side. It is essentially the same
motif, except it's a triangle instead of
a square.

With color, ch 4, 2 dc in 4th ch from
hook, ch 5, pull lp through first dc,
in ch-5 sp make 5 sc, dc in 2nd dc
of 2nd group of 3-dc group from
joining of 2 Large Motifs, 2 sc in
same ch-5 sp, dc in same ch as beg
2-dc, ch 1, sc in next ch-3 sp on
Large Motif, ch 1, 3 dc in same ch
as beg 2-dc, ch 5, pull lp through
first dc of 3-dc group just made, 2
sc in ch-5 sp just made, dc in 2nd
of 3-dc group close to joining of 2
Large Motifs, 3 sc in same ch-5 sp,
dc in next 2nd dc of 3-dc group of
next Large Motif, 2 sc in same ch-5
sp, dc in same first ch of beg ch-4, ch
1, sc in next ch-3 sp on Large Motif,
ch 1, 3 dc in same ch as beg 2-dc,
ch 5, pull lp through first dc of 3-dc

group, 2 sc in ch-5 sp, dc in 2nd dc of 3-dc group on Large Motif, 5 sc in same ch-5 sp, dc in same ch as beg 2-dc, ch 4, join with sl st in 3rd ch of beg ch-4. Fasten off.

BORDER
Rnd 1: Join aran in any corner ch-3 sp of shell of Large Motif, ch 4 *(counts as first tr)*, (ch 3, tr) 4 times in same corner ch-3 sp, *[ch 3, (dc, {ch 2, dc} 3 times) in next ch-3 sp] twice**, ch 3, (dc, ch 3, dc) in **back lp** *(see Stitch Guide)* only of 3rd sc of 5-sc group, (dc, ch 3, dc) in back lp of 2nd ch of next ch-3 sp, (dc, ch 3, dc) in back lp of 3rd sc of next 5-sc group, rep from * across edge to next corner ch-3 sp, ending last rep across edge at**, (ch 3, tr) 5 times in corner ch-3 sp, rep from * around outer edge, ending final rep at **, ch 3, join with sl st in 4th ch of beg ch-4.

Rnd 2: Sl st into ch-3 sp, ch 1, (sc, ch 3, sc) in each of next 4 corner ch-3 sps, *[sc in next ch-3 sp, (sc, ch 3, sc) in each of next 3 ch-3 sps] twice, sc in next ch-3 sp**, [(sc, ch 3, sc) in next ch-3 sp, sc in 2nd dc] twice, (sc, ch 3, sc) in next ch-3 sp, rep from * across edge, ending last rep at ** before 4-corner ch-3 sps, (sc, ch 3, sc) in each of 4 corner ch-3 sps, rep from * around, ending final rep at **, join with sl st in beg sc. Fasten off. ❏❏

Happy Times

Design by Dot Drake

SKILL LEVEL

BEGINNER

FINISHED SIZE
40 x 70 inches

MATERIALS
- ❑ Medium (worsted) weight yarn:
  3 oz/150 yds/85g white
  2 oz/100 yds/57g for each
  CC used
- ❑ Size H/8/5mm crochet hook or size needed to obtain gauge

GAUGE
13 hdc = 4 inches, 8 hdc rows = 4 inches

SPECIAL STITCH
Picot: Ch 5, sl st in 4th ch from hook.

INSTRUCTIONS
AFGHAN
Row 1: With white, work **picot** *(see Special Stitch)* 114 times, turn.

Row 2: Ch 2 *(counts as first hdc throughout)*, [hdc in next ch between picots, hdc in ch at base of next picot] across, ending with hdc in last ch after last picot, turn. Fasten off white. *(228 hdc)*

Row 3: Join first CC with sl st in first st of last row, ch 2, hdc in each st across, turn. *(228 hdc)*

Row 4: Ch 2, hdc in each st across, turn. Fasten off.

Row 5: Join next CC with sl st in first st of last row, ch 1, sc in first st, [tr in next st, sc in next st] across to last st, sc in last st, turn. Fasten off. *(228 sts)*

Row 6: Join CC with sl st in first st of last row, ch 2, hdc in each st across, turn. *(228 hdc)*

Row 7: Ch 2, hdc in each st across, turn. Fasten off.

Rows 8–12: Rep rows 3–7 with next 2 desired CCs.

Next rows: Rep rows 8–12 until Afghan measures approximately 40 inches.

Next row: Join white with sl st in first st, ch 2, hdc in each st across, turn.

Last row: Sl st in first hdc, [ch 3, sl st in 3rd ch from hook, sl st in each of next 2 hdc] across to last st, sl st in last st. Fasten off. ❏❏

Colored Chalk

Design by Darla Fanton

SKILL LEVEL

■ ■ ■ ▢

INTERMEDIATE

FINISHED SIZES
47 x 71 inches

MATERIALS
- ❑ Red Heart Super Saver medium (worsted) weight yarn:
  25 oz/1250 yds/709g
  #312 black
  2 oz/100 yds/57g each
  15 assorted scrap colors
- ❑ Size K/10½/6.5mm flexible double-ended crochet hook or size needed to obtain gauge
- ❑ Size K/10½/6.5mm crochet hook

GAUGE
With double-ended hook: 25 sts = 4¼ inches, 13 rows = 3 inches

SPECIAL STITCHES
Change color: Place sl knot on hook, pull sl knot through first lp on hook.

Single crochet loop (sc lp): Insert hook in next ch, yo, pull lp through, yo, pull through 1 lp on hook.

INSTRUCTIONS
AFGHAN
Row 1: With double-ended hook, ch 278, working in **back bar of ch** (see illustration) and leaving all lps on hook, pull up lp in 2nd ch from hook and in each ch across, turn hook and slide sts to opposite end of hook, **do not fasten off.** (278 lps on hook)

Back Bar of Chain

Row 2: Change to scrap color (see Special Stitches), to work lps off hook, [yo, pull through 2 lps on hook] across, do not turn. Last lp on hook, is first st of next row.

Row 3: Ch 1, sk first vertical bar, 3 **sc lps** (see Special Stitches) in next **vertical bar** (see illustration), sc lp in each of next 10 vertical bars, sk next 4 vertical bars, sc lp in each of next 10 vertical bars, [5 sc lps in next vertical bar, sc lp in each of next 10 vertical bars, sk next 4 vertical bars, sc lp in each of next 10 vertical bars] across to last 2 vertical bars, 3 sc lps in next vertical bar, sc lp in last vertical bar, **turn hook**. Fasten off. (278 lps)

Vertical Bar

Horizontal Bar

Row 4: With black, yo, pull through 1 lp on hook, [yo, pull through 2 lps on hook] 11 times, yo, pull through 5 lps on hook (cl), *[yo, pull through 2 lps on hook] 21 times, yo pull through 5 lps (cl), rep from* 9 times, [yo, pull through 2 lps on hook] 12 times, do not turn. (1 lp)

Row 5: Ch 1, sk first vertical bar, pull up lp in next vertical bar, pull up lp in next **horizontal bar** (see illustration), pull up lp in next vertical bar,*[yo, sk next horizontal bar, pick up lp in next horizontal bar] 5 times, sk cl, [yo, pick up lp in next horizontal bar, sk next horizontal bar] 5 times, [pick up lp in next vertical bar, pick up lp in next horizontal bar] twice**, pick up lp in next vertical bar, rep from *, ending last rep at **, **turn hook**. (278 lps)

Row 6: Change to next scrap color, [yo, pull through 2 lps on hook] across, do not turn. (1 lp)

Rows 7–244: Rep rows 3–6 consecutively, ending with row 4.

Row 245: Ch 1, sk first horizontal bar, sl st in each horizontal bar across. **Do not fasten off.**

Edging
Row 246: Working in ends of rows down side, with crochet hook and black, ch 2, evenly sp hdc across so piece lies flat to end of row 1, ch 2, sl st in end of row 1. Fasten off.

Row 247: Working in ends of rows on opposite side, with crochet hook, join black with sl st in end of row 1, ch 2, evenly sp hdc across so piece lies flat to last row, ch 2, sl st in last row. Fasten off. ❑❑

Summer Colors

Design by Hazel Henry

SKILL LEVEL

INTERMEDIATE

FINISHED SIZE
Blocked: 15 inches across

MATERIALS
❑ Crochet cotton size 10:
   150 yds green
   35 yds pink
   20 yds blue
   15 yds yellow
❑ Size 9/1.25mm steel crochet hook or size needed to obtain gauge

GAUGE
Rnds 1 & 2 = 2 inches across

SPECIAL STITCHES
Beginning cluster (beg cl): Ch 4, *yo twice, insert hook in same ch sp, yo, pull lp through, [yo, pull through 2 lps on hook] twice, rep from *, yo, pull through all lps on hook.

Cluster (cl): *Yo twice, insert hook in ch sp, yo, pull lp through, [yo, pull through 2 lps on hook] twice, rep from * twice in same ch sp, yo, pull through all lps on hook.

Picot cluster (picot cl): Ch 4, sl st in 4th ch from hook, [ch 4, sl st in same ch] twice, *ch 6, sl st in 4th ch from hook, [ch 4, sl st in same ch] twice, rep from *, sl st in same ch as first beg ch-4.

Beginning cluster shell (beg cl shell): Ch 4, yo twice, insert hook in same st, *yo, pull lp through, [yo, pull through 2 lps on hook] twice*, yo twice, insert hook in next tr, rep between *, yo, pull through all lps on hook, ch 3, [yo twice, insert hook in same tr as last st made, rep between *, yo twice, insert hook in next tr, rep between *] rep between [ ], yo, pull through all lps on hook, ch 3, rep between [ ], yo twice, insert hook in same tr as last st made, rep

between *, yo, pull through all lps on hook.

Cluster shell (cl shell): Yo twice, insert hook in next tr, yo, pull lp through, [yo, pull through 2 lps on hook] twice, yo twice, insert hook in same st, *yo, pull lp through, [yo, pull through 2 lps on hook] twice*, yo twice, insert hook in next tr, rep between *, yo, pull through all lps on hook, ch 3, [yo twice, insert hook in same tr as last st made, rep between *, yo twice, insert hook in next tr, rep between *] rep between [ ], yo, pull through all lps on hook, ch 3, rep between [ ], yo twice, insert hook in same tr as last st made, rep between *, yo, pull through all lps on hook.

INSTRUCTIONS
DOILY
Rnd 1: With green, ch 12, sl st in first ch to form ring, ch 1, 24 sc in ring, join with sl st in beg sc. *(24 sc)*

Rnd 2: Ch 3 *(counts as first dc throughout)*, dc in same st, 2 dc in each st around, join with sl st in 3rd ch of beg ch-3. *(48 dc)*

Rnd 3: Ch 5 *(counts as first dc and ch 2)*, sk next st, [dc in next st, ch 2, sk next st] around, join with sl st in 3rd ch of beg ch-5. *(24 dc, 24 ch-2 sps)*

Rnd 4: Ch 6 *(counts as first dc and ch 3)*, [dc in next dc, ch 3] around, join with sl st in 3rd ch of beg ch-6.

Rnd 5: Ch 4 *(counts as first tr throughout)*, tr in same st, ch 4, [2 tr in next dc, ch 4] around, join with sl st in 4th ch of beg ch-4. *(48 dc, 48 ch-4 sps)*

Rnd 6: Sl st in next st, sl st in first ch sp, (**beg cl**—*see Special Stitches*, ch 5, **cl**—*see Special Stitches*) in same ch sp, ch 7, sk next ch sp, *(cl, ch 5, cl) in next ch sp, ch 7, sk next ch sp, rep from * around, join with sl st in top of beg cl. *(24 cls, 12 ch-7 sps, 12 ch-5 sps)*

Rnd 7: Ch 1, sc in first st, *ch 11, sl st in 7th ch from hook, ch 4, sc in top of next cl, 7 sc in ch-7 sp**, sc in top of next cl, rep from * around, ending last rep at **, join with sl st in first sc. Fasten off.

Rnd 8: Join yellow with sl st in any ch-6 sp, beg cl, *(ch 3, cl) 5 times in same ch sp, sk next 4 sc, (dc, ch 3, dc) in next sc**, cl in next ch-6 sp, rep from * around, ending last rep at ** join with sl st in top of beg cl. Fasten off. *(72 ch-3 sps)*

Rnd 9: Join green with sc in any ch-3 sp between dc, 3 sc in same ch sp, 4 sc in each ch-3 sp around, join with sl st in beg sc. *(288 sc)*

Rnd 10: Ch 4, *sk next 2 sc, tr in next sc, ch 2, sk next 3 sc, sc in next sc, [ch 5, sk next 3 sc, sc in next sc] 3 times, ch 2, sk next 4 sc**, tr in next sc, rep from * around, ending last rep at **, join with sl st in 4th ch of beg ch-4. *(36 ch-3 sps, 24 tr, 24 ch-2 sps)*

Rnd 11: Ch 6, tr in next tr, ch 2, *sk next ch-2 sp, dc in 3rd ch of next ch-5 sp, [ch 3, dc in next sc, ch 3, dc in 3rd ch of next ch-5 sp] twice**, ch 2, sk next ch-2 sp, [tr in next tr, ch 2] twice, rep from * around, ending last rep at **, join with hdc in 4th ch of beg ch-6, **turn,** sl st in last dc made, **turn.**

Rnd 12: Ch 4, tr in same st, *ch 7, sk next 2 tr, [2 tr in next dc, ch 7, sk next dc] twice**, 2 tr in next in next dc, rep from * around, ending last rep at **, join with sl st in 4th ch of beg ch-4. *(36 ch-7 sps)*

Rnd 13: Sl st in next tr, sl st in next ch sp, ch 1, (sc, 2 hdc, 2 dc, 2 hdc, sc) in each ch-7 sp around, join with sl st in beg sc. Fasten off.

Rnd 14: Join blue with sl st in last st on last rnd, ch 4, tr in next st, *ch 4, sk next 2 sts, sc in each of next 2 sts, ch 4, sk next 2 sts, tr in next st, **picot cl** (see Special Stitches), tr in next st, ch 4, sk next 2 sts, sc in each of next 2 sts, ch 4, sk next 2 sts, tr in each of next 2 sts, ch 4, sk next 2 sts, sc in next st, picot cl, sc in next st, ch 4, sk next 2 sts**, tr in each of next 2 sts, rep from * around, ending last rep at **, join with sl st in 4th ch of beg ch-4. Fasten off. *(24 picot cls)*

Rnd 15: Join green with sc in center ch-4 sp of any picot cl, ch 15, [sc in center ch-4 sp of next picot cl, ch 15] around, join with sl st in beg sc. *(24 ch-15 sps)*

Rnd 16: Sl st in first ch, ch 4, tr in same ch, ch 3, tr in next ch, sk next 3 chs, [2 tr in next ch, ch 3, tr in next ch, sk next 3 chs] twice, sk next sc, *2 tr in next ch, ch 3, tr in next ch, sk next 3 chs, [2 tr in next ch, ch 3, tr in next ch, sk next 3 chs] twice, sk next sc, rep from * around, join with sl st in 4th ch of beg ch-4.

Rnd 17: Ch 4, tr in next tr, sk next ch sp, tr in next tr, ch 4, *tr in each of next 2 tr, sk next ch sp, tr in next tr, ch 4, rep from * around, join with sl st in 4th ch of beg ch-4.

Rnd 18: Ch 4, tr in next tr, ch 5, tr in next tr, sk next ch sp, *tr in each of next 2 tr, ch 5, tr in next tr, sk next ch sp, rep from * around, join with sl

st in top of beg ch-4. Fasten off.

Rnd 19: Join pink with sl st in any ch sp, ch 4, 4 tr in same ch sp, ch 5, sc in next ch sp, ch 5, *5 tr in next ch sp, ch 5, sc in next ch-2 sp, ch 5, rep from * around, join with sl st in 4th ch of beg ch-4.

Rnd 20: Beg cl shell (see Special Stitches), ch 9, sk next 2 ch sps, ***cl shell** (see Special Stitches), ch 9, sk next 2 ch sps, rep from * around, join with sl st in top of beg cl shell. Fasten off. *(36 cl shells)*

Rnd 21: Join green with sc in any ch-9 sp, 8 sc in same ch sp, 3 sc in each ch-3 sp and 9 sc in each ch-9 sp around, join with sl st in beg sc.

Rnd 22: Sl st in each of next 4 sts, ch 1, sc in same st, ch 5, sk next 6 sts, tr in next st, ch 3, tr in next st, ch 5, sk next 6 sts, [sc in next st, ch 5, sk next 6 sts, tr in next st, ch 3, tr in next st, ch 5, sk next 6 sts] around, join with sl st in beg sc.

Rnd 23: Ch 7, tr in same st, ch 7, sk next ch-5 sp, sc in next ch-3 sp, ch 7, sk next ch-5 sp, *(tr, ch 3, tr) in next sc, ch 7, sk next ch-5 sp, sc in next ch-3 sp, ch 7, sk next ch-5 sp, rep from * around, join with sl st in 4th ch of beg ch-7.

Rnd 24: Sl st in each of next 2 chs, ch 9, sl st in 4th ch from hook, ch 1, tr in same ch, *ch 8, sk next ch-7 sp, sc in next sc, ch 8, sk next ch-7 sp**, (tr, ch 5, sl st in 4th ch from hook, ch 1, tr) in next ch-3 sp, rep from * around, ending last rep at **, join with sl st in 4th ch of beg ch-9. Fasten off. ❑❑

Starburst

Design by Kathleen Garen

SKILL LEVEL

INTERMEDIATE

FINISHED SIZE

Fits 16-inch-diameter pillow form

MATERIALS

- ❑ Medium (worsted) weight yarn:
    Small amounts various colors
    as desired
- ❑ Size H/8/5mm crochet hook or
    size needed to obtain gauge
- ❑ Tapestry needle
- ❑ 16-inch round pillow form

GAUGE

4 dc = 1 inch; 3 dc rnds = 2 inches

PATTERN NOTES

Pillow is crocheted from the outside toward the center. Round 10 will be the central star of the design. Choose colors with this in mind.

Any number or combinations of colors may be used, with varying patterns emerging.

Use a different color for each round unless otherwise indicated.

INSTRUCTIONS

PILLOW
Side
Make 2.

Rnd 1: Ch 160, using care not to twist ch, sl st to join in beg ch to form circle, ch 3 *(counts as first dc)*, dc in each of next 9 chs, ch 11, [dc in each of next 10 chs, ch 11] 15 times, join with sl st in 3rd ch of beg ch-3. Fasten off. *(16 groups 10 dc, 16 ch-11 lps)*

Rnd 2: Working in **back lps** *(see Stitch Guide)* only, sk first st of any dc group, join with sl st in next st, ch 1, sc in same st, ch 2 *(sc and ch-2 counts as first dc)*, dc in each st across group, ch 11, [sk first dc of next group, dc in each st across group, ch 11] around, join with sl st in 2nd ch of beg ch-2. Fasten off.

Rnds 3–8: Rep rnd 2. *(At the end of last rnd, 3 dc each group)*

Rnd 9: Working in back lps only, sk first st of any dc group, join with sl st in next st, ch 1, sc in same st, ch 2, dc in back lp of next st, **do not ch 11**, dc in back lp of 2nd and 3rd sts of next group, ch 11, [dc in back lp of 2nd and 3rd sts of next group of each of next 2 groups, ch 11] around, join with sl st in 2nd ch of beg ch-2. Fasten off. *(8 groups 4-dc, 8 ch-11 lps)*

Weaving Loops

Starting with any 4-dc section, beg joining lps, give the lp from rnd 1 only a half twist *(to eliminate a hole at that spot)*, then pull lp from rnd 2 through lp of rnd 1, pull lp from rnd 3, through lp of rnd 2, continue to rep until lp from rnd 8 is pulled through lp of rnd 7. Rep joining lps of the rem 7 sections of each 4-dc group.

Rnd 10: Working in back lps only, join next yarn color with sl st in 2nd st of any 4-dc group, ch 1, sc in same st, working through lp of rnd 8 to secure it, ch 2, dc in back lp of next st and also working through lp, sk last dc, ch 11, [dc in 2nd and 3rd sts of next group, catching in lp of rnd 8, ch 11] around, join with sl st in beg sc, **do not fasten off.**

Rnd 11: Ch 2, dc in next st, **do not ch**, [**dc dec** *(see Stitch Guide)* in next 2 sts, do not ch] around, join with sl st in top of first dc. Fasten off.

Final Weave
Weave lps of rem section as before until lp of rnd 10 is pulled through rnd 9 on each of the rem section to be woven.

Cut a 6-inch length of yarn the same color as used in rnd 11, weave through rem lps of rnd 10, gather lps tightly tog, knot to secure, pass ends of yarn to WS of Pillow and secure.

Finishing
Rnd 1: With WS of Pillow Sides tog, working through both thicknesses in starting ch on of opposite side of rnd 1, join with sl st in any ch, ch 1, sc in same ch, ch 3, sk next ch, [sc in next ch, ch 3, sk next ch] around insert pillow form before closing, join with sl st in beg sc. Fasten off.

Rnd 2: Working in sk chs of opposite side of starting ch, join next color with sl st in first sk ch, ch 1, sc in same ch, ch 3, [sc in next sk ch, ch 3] around, join with sl st in beg sc. Fasten off. ❑❑

Bag Lady
Design by Sue Collins Ottinger

FINISHED SIZE
15 inches tall

MATERIALS
- ❑ Medium (worsted) weight yarn: small amount each skin tone, tan for bag Assorted colors for dress and hat
- ❑ Size G/6/4mm crochet hook or size needed to obtain gauge
- ❑ Size F/5/3.75mm crochet hook
- ❑ Tapestry needle
- ❑ Sewing needle
- ❑ 1 pair 9mm eyes
- ❑ ½-inch red button for mouth
- ❑ 3 (⅜ inch) buttons for dress
- ❑ Plastic bags
- ❑ Thin metallic elastic cord
- ❑ Sewing thread or craft glue

GAUGE
Size G hook: 10 dc = 3 inches

PATTERN NOTES
Change color *(see Stitch Guide)* in last stitch made.

Do not join rounds unless otherwise stated; mark first stitch of each round with safety pin or other small marker.

SPECIAL STITCH
Double crochet cluster (dc cl): Holding back on hook last lp of each st, 2 dc in indicated st, yo, pull through all lps on hook.

INSTRUCTIONS
BAG LADY
Head
Rnd 1: With size G hook and skin tone, ch 2, 6 sc in 2nd ch from hook, **do not join** (see Pattern Notes). (6 sc)

Rnd 2: 2 sc in each st around. (12 sc)

Rnd 3: [2 sc in next st, sc in next st] around. (18 sc)

Rnd 4: Sc in each st around.

Rnd 5: [2 sc in next st, sc in each of next 2 sts] around. (24 sc)

Rnds 6 & 7: Sc in each st around.

Rnd 8: [2 sc in next st, sc in each of next 3 sts] around. (30 sc)

Rnd 9: Sc in each st around.

Rnd 10: Sc in each of first 15 sts, **dc cl** (see Special Stitch) in next st for nose, sc in each of last 14 sts. (30 sts)

Rnd 11: Sc in each of first 14 sts, **sc dec** (see Stitch Guide) in next 2 sts, sc in each of last 14 sts. (29 sts)

Rnd 12: Sc in each st around. (29 sc)

Rnd 13: Sc in each of first 2 sts, *sc dec in next 2 sts, sc in next st, sc dec in next 2 sts**, sc in each of next 2 sts, rep from * around, ending last rep at **, sc in last st. (21 sts)

Rnd 14: Sc in each st around.

Rnd 15: [Sc dec in next 2 sts, sc in each of next 2 sts] around to last st, sc in last st. (16 sts)

Rnd 16: [Sc dec in next 2 sts, sc in each of next 2 sts] around. (12 sts)

Rnds 17 & 18: Sc in each st around, **change to dress color** (see Pattern Notes) in last sc of rnd 18.

Dress
Note: When working dress, change colors whenever desired.

Rnd 1: 2 hdc in each st around. (24 hdc)

Rnd 2: Hdc in each of next 21 sts, sc in each of next 2 sts, sl st in next st, **turn.**

Rnd 3: Ch 2 (counts as first hdc throughout), hdc in each of next 2 sts, [2 hdc in next st, hdc in each of next 2 sts] around, join with sl st in 2nd ch of beg ch-2, **turn.** (31 hdc)

Rnds 4–13: Ch 2, hdc in each st around, join with sl st in top of beg ch-2, **turn.**

Rnd 14: Ch 3 (counts as first dc throughout), dc in same st, 2 dc in each st around, join with sl st in top of beg ch-3, **turn.** (62 dc)

Rnds 15–27: Ch 3, dc in each st around, join with sl st in top of beg ch-3, **turn.**

Rnd 28: Ch 3, dc in each st around, join with sl st in top of beg ch-3, **do not turn.**

Rnd 29: Working in **front lps** (see Stitch Guide) only this rnd, ch 3, 3 dc in same st, 4 dc in each st around, join with sl st in top of beg ch-3. Fasten off.

Rnd 30: Join with sl st in first rem lp of last rnd, ch 2, sk next st, [hdc in next st, sk next st] around, join with sl st in top of beg ch-2. Fasten off.

Hand & Arm
Make 2.

Rnd 1: With size G hook and skin tone, ch 2, 6 sc in 2nd ch from hook. (6 sc)

Rnds 2–4: Sc in each st around, changing to dress color in last sc of rnd 4.

Rnd 5: [2 sc in each of next 2 sts, sc in next st] around. (10 sc)

Rnds 6–23: Sc in each st around.

Rnd 24: [Sc in each of next 2 sts, sc dec in next 2 sts] twice, sc in each of last 2 sts, join with sl st in beg sc. Fasten off.

HAT
Note: Change colors whenever desired.

Rnd 1: With G hook, ch 2, 6 sc in 2nd ch from hook. (6 sc)

Rnd 2: 3 dc in each st around. (18 dc)

Rnd 3: 3 dc in each st around (54 dc)

Rnds 4–6: Dc in each st around.

Rnd 7: [**Dc dec** (see Stitch Guide) in next 2 sts] around. (27 sts)

Rnd 8: Working in **back lps** (see Stitch Guide) only around, 3 tr in each of next 27 sts, hdc in next st, sc in next st, sl st in next st. Fasten off.

SHOPPING BAG
Rnd 1: With size F hook and tan, ch 9, sc in 2nd ch from hook and in each of next 6 chs, 3 sc in last ch; working across opposite side of ch, sc in each of next 6 chs, 2 sc in last ch. (18 sc)

Rnd 2: 2 sc in next st, sc in each of next 6 sts, 2 sc in next st, sc in next st, 2 sc in next st, sc in each of next 6 sts, 2 sc in next st, sc in next st. (22 sc)

Rnd 3: Working in back lps only this rnd, sc in each st around.

Rnds 4–10: Sc in each st around; **do not fasten off** at end of last rnd.

Handles
Sl st in each of first 3 sts, ch 10, **turn,** sk last 3 sl sts and next 3 sc, sl st in next sc. Fasten off.

Sk next 4 unworked sc on last rnd, join tan with sl st in next st, ch 10, sk next 5 sts, sl st in next st. Fasten off.

FINISHING
1. Sew or glue eyes to Head 1 rnd above nose. Sew red button below nose. Stuff Head with plastic bag. Stuff upper body with plastic bags.

2. Thread yarn needle with 2 lengths of yarn, each 18 inches. Flatten upper body at rnd 13. Beg at either side of waist and leaving a 5-inch end, weave front and back sts of flattened rnd 13 tog. Knot ends of thread at each side of waist tog and tie into bows. Trim ends or let hang down as desired.

3. With yarn needle and yarn, sew 3 buttons down front of upper Dress.

4. Weave length of metallic elastic cord through sts of rnd 7 of Hat. Place Hat on Head, pull cord tight, double-knot and tie into bow. With yarn needle and same color yarn as Hat ruffle, tack center front and center back of Hat to Head.

5. Weave rem length of metallic elastic cord through last rnd of skirt. Leaving an opening large enough for a fist, double-knot cord and trim ends.

6. Stuff each Arm lightly with a plastic bag or part of a plastic bag. Flatten last rnd of each Arm and sew to top of Dress on each side. With yarn needle and matching yarn, tack Arms to waist at each side, leaving short ends visible at front of each arm.

7. Tack Handles of shopping bag to hands.

Hanger
With F hook and tan, make a ch approximately 9 inches in length. Thread through st of rnd 2 of Hat at top center. Tie ends tog.

Stuff skirt with plastic shopping bags. ❏❏

Spring Baskets

Design by Lucille LaFlamme

FINISHED SIZE

11 x 19½ inches after blocking

MATERIALS

- ❑ Crochet cotton size 10:
    - 300 yds white
    - 36 yds light pink
    - 24 yds pink
    - 20 yds light green
    - 12 yds each light blue, blue and yellow
- ❑ Size 6/1.80mm steel crochet hook or size needed to obtain gauge
- ❑ Tapestry needle
- ❑ Sewing needle
- ❑ White sewing thread

GAUGE

41 tr and chs = 4 inches, 9 tr rows = 4 inches

SPECIAL STITCHES

Shell: (2 dc, ch 2, 2 dc) in next ch sp.

V-stitch (V-st): (Dc, ch 3, dc) in next ch sp.

Picot: Ch 4, sl st in last st made.

Treble crochet cluster (tr cl): *Yo twice, insert hook in ring, yo, pull lp through, [yo, pull through 2 lps on hook] twice, rep from * twice, yo, pull through all lps on hook.

INSTRUCTIONS

MAT

Row 1: With white, ch 117, tr in 5th ch from hook *(first 4 chs count as first tr)*, [ch 5, sk next 5 chs, tr in each of next 2 chs] across, turn. *(34 tr, 16 ch sps)*

Row 2: Ch 4 *(count as first tr)*, tr in next st, [ch 5, sc in next ch sp, ch 5, tr in each of next 2 sts] across, turn. *(34 tr, 32 ch sps, 16 sc)*

Rows 3 & 4: Ch 4, tr in next tr, [ch 5, sk next 2 ch sps, tr in each of next 2 tr] across, turn.

Rows 5–28: Rep rows 2–4 consecutively. At end of last row, fasten off.

BASKET

Make 2.

Row 1: With white, ch 30, dc in 4th ch from hook *(first 3 chs count as first dc)* and in each ch across, turn. *(28 dc)*

Row 2: Ch 3 *(counts as first dc throughout)*, dc in each of next 3 sts, [ch 1, dc in each of next 4 sts] across, turn. *(28 dc, 6 ch sps)*

Row 3: Ch 3, dc in each of next 3 dc, [ch 3, dc in each of next 4 dc] across, turn.

Row 4: Ch 1, sc in first st, ch 3, sk next 2 sts, sc in next st, [ch 3, sc in next ch sp, ch 3, sc in next st, ch 3, sk next 2 sts, sc in next st] across, turn. *(20 sc, 19 ch sps)*

Row 5: Ch 3, (dc, ch 2, 2 dc) in next ch sp, ch 3, sc in next ch sp, ch 2, [**shell** (see Special Stitches), ch 2, sc in next ch sp, ch 3, sc in next ch sp, ch 2] across to last ch sp, shell in last ch sp, dc in last st, turn. *(12 sc, 12 ch-2 sps, 6 ch-3 sps, 7 shells)*

Row 6: Ch 3, shell, [ch 3, sk next ch sp, sc in next ch sp, ch 3, sk next ch sp, shell] across with dc in top of ch-3, turn. *(12 ch sps, 7 shells, 2 dc)*

Row 7: Ch 1, sc in each of first 3 sts, sc in next ch sp, [ch 7, sk next 2 ch sps, sc in next ch sp] across with sc in each of last 3 sts, turn. *(13 sc, 6 ch sps)*

Row 8: Ch 3, dc in each of next 3 sts, ch 3, 3 dc in 4th ch of next ch-7, ch 3, [dc in next sc, ch 3, 3 dc in 4th ch of next ch-7, ch 3] across with dc in each of last 4 sts, turn. *(31 dc, 12 ch sps)*

Row 9: Ch 3, dc in each of next 3 dc, ch 5, **dc dec** (see Stitch Guide) in next 3 sts, [ch 3, 3 dc in next dc, ch 3, dc dec in next 3 sts] across to last 4 sts, ch 5, dc in each of last 4 sts, turn. *(29 dc, 10 ch-3 sps, 2 ch-5 sps)*

Row 10: Ch 3, dc in each of next 3 sts, ch 5, dc dec in next 3 sts, [ch 3, dc dec in next 3 sts, ch 3, dc in next dc dec] across with ch 5, dc in each of last 4 sts, turn. *(19 dc, 10 ch-3 sps, 2 ch-5 sps)*

Row 11: Ch 3, dc in each of next 3 sts, ch 3, shell in next dc, ch 3, [sk next dc dec, shell in next dc, ch 3] across with dc in each of last 4 sts, turn. *(8 dc, 7 ch-3 sps, 6 shells)*

Row 12: Ch 3, dc in each of next 3 sts, ch 5, shell in next shell, [ch 3, shell in next shell] across with ch 5, dc in each of last 4 sts, turn. *(8 dc, 6 shells, 5 ch-3 sps, 2 ch-5 sps)*

Row 13: Ch 3, dc in each of next 3 sts, ch 3, dc in next ch sp, ch 3, [**V-st** (see Special Stitches), ch 3, dc in next ch sp, ch 3] across with dc in each of last 4 sts, turn. *(15 dc, 14 ch-3 sps, 6 V-sts)*

Row 14: Ch 3, dc in each of next 3 sts, ch 3, sc in next dc, **picot** (see Special Stitches), ch 3, *(3 dc, picot, 3 dc) in next V-st, ch 3, sc in next dc, picot, ch 3, rep from * across with dc in each of last 4 sts, turn.

Row 15: For **handle**, ch 3, dc in each of next 3 sts leaving rem sts unworked, turn. *(4 dc)*

Rows 16–65: Ch 3, dc in each of last 3 sts, turn. At end of last row, fasten off.

Matching sts, sew row 65 to last 4 sts on row 14.

Sew row 14 and Handle of 1 Basket over center of rows 1–11 of Mat and row 14 and Handle of 2nd Basket over center of rows 18–28 of Mat as shown in photo.

ROSE
Make 6 light pink.
Make 4 pink.

Rnd 1: Ch 6, sl st in first ch to form ring, ch 1, (sc, ch 3) 6 times in ring, join with sl st in beg sc. *(6 sc, 6 ch sps)*

Rnd 2: Sl st in first ch sp, ch 1, (sc, hdc, dc, hdc, sc) in each ch sp around, join with sl st in beg sc. *(6 petals)*

Rnd 3: Ch 4, sk next petal, [sl st in next sc on rnd 1, ch 4, sk next petal] around, join with sl st in first ch of beg ch-4. *(6 ch sps)*

Rnd 4: Ch 1, (sc, hdc, dc, 2 tr, dc, hdc, sc) in each ch sp around, join with sl st in beg sc. Fasten off.

MEDIUM FLOWER
Make 4 blue.
Make 4 light blue.

Ch 6, sl st in first ch to form ring, [ch 4, **tr cl** (see Special Stitches), ch 3, sl st in top of tr cl just made, ch 4, sc) 5 times in ring, join with sl st in first ch of beg ch-4. Fasten off.

SMALL FLOWER
Make 6.

With yellow, ch 6, sl st in first ch to form ring, ch 1, [sc, ch 4, sc, ch 8] 5 times in ring, join with sl st in beg sc. Fasten off.

LEAF
Make 8.

With light green, ch 15, sc in 2nd ch from hook, *hdc in next ch, dc in each of next 3 chs, tr in each of next 4 chs, dc in each of next 3 chs, hdc in next ch, sc in last ch* ch 3, working on opposite side of ch, sc in next ch, rep between *, join with sl st in beg sc. Fasten off.

Sew Roses, Flowers and leaves across Mat and Flower Baskets as shown in photo or as desired. ❑❑

Butterfly's Fancy Table Set

Designs by Maggie Petsch

SKILL LEVEL

INTERMEDIATE

FINISHED SIZES

Place Mat: 12½ x 16 inches
Napkin Ring: 2¼ inches wide

MATERIALS

- ❑ Crochet cotton size 3 (100 yds per ball):
  - 1 ball white
  - ½ ball each black, yellow, green and rose
- ❑ Size D/3/3.25 crochet hook or size needed to obtain gauge
- ❑ Tapestry needle

GAUGE

Rnds 1 and 2 of Head = 1¼ inches in diameter

SPECIAL STITCHES

Joined loop (joined lp): Ch 2, sl st in indicated lp, ch 2.

3-double crochet cluster (dc cl): Holding back on hook last lp of each st, 3 dc in indicated st, yo, pull through all lps on hook.

Beginning 3-treble crochet cluster (beg tr cl): Ch 3, holding back on hook last lp of each st, 2 tr in same st, yo, pull through all lps on hook.

3-treble crochet cluster (tr cl): Holding back on hook last lp of each st, 3 tr in indicated st, yo, pull through all lps on hook.

Beginning split cluster (beg split cl): Ch 3, holding back on hook last lp of each st, tr in same st, 2 tr in next st, yo, pull through all lps on hook.

Split cluster (split cl): Holding back on hook last lp of each st, 2 tr in each of next 2 sts, yo, pull through all lps on hook.

RUCTIONS

Head

Rnd 1: With black, ch 4, 11 dc in 4th ch from hook *(first 3 chs count as first dc)*, join with sl st in 4th ch of beg ch-4. *(12 dc)*

Rnd 2: Ch 3 *(counts as first dc throughout)*, dc in same st, 2 dc in each dc around, join with sl st in 3rd ch of beg ch-3. *(24 dc)*

Body

Row 1 (RS): Ch 3, 4 dc in same st leaving rem sts unworked, turn. *(5 dc)*

Rows 2–34: Ch 2 *(counts as first hdc)*, hdc in each of next 4 sts, turn. *(5 hdc)*

Row 35: Ch 2, **dc dec** *(see Stitch Guide)* in next 4 sts. Fasten off.

Upper Left Wing

Rnd 1 (RS): With white, ch 2, 6 sc in 2nd ch from hook, join with sl st in beg sc. *(6 sc)*

Rnd 2: Ch 1, 2 sc in same st as joining, 2 sc in each sc around, join with sl st in beg sc. Fasten off. *(12 sc)*

Rnd 3: With RS facing, join rose with sl st in any sc, **beg split cl** *(see Special Stitches)*, ch 7, [**split cl** *(see Special Stitches)*, ch 7] around, join with sl st in top of beg split cl. Fasten off.

Rnd 4: With RS facing, join green with sl st in top of any split cl, **beg tr cl** *(see Special Stitches)* in same st, ch 3, *(**dc cl**–*see Special Stitches,* ch 3, dc cl) in 4th ch of next ch-7, ch 3**, **tr cl** *(see Special Stitches)* in next split cl, ch 3, rep from * around, ending last rep at **, join with sl st in top of beg tr cl. Fasten off.

Rnd 5: With RS facing, join yellow with sl st in any ch-3 sp, ch 6, [sl st in next ch sp, ch 6] around, join with sl st in same ch sp as beg sl st. Fasten off.

Lower Left Wing

Rnds 1 & 2: Rep rnds 1 and 2 of Upper Left Wing; at end of rnd 2, **do not fasten off.**

Rnd 3: Ch 1, sc in first st, 2 sc in next sc, [sc in next sc, 2 sc in next sc] around, join with sl st in beg sc. Fasten off. *(18 sc)*

Rnd 4: With RS facing, join rose with sl st in any sc, ch 1, sc in same st, [sc in next sc of rnd 1, sc in each of next 3 sc on working rnd] 5 times, sc in next sc of rnd 1, sc in each of next 2 sc, join with sl st in beg sc. *(24 sc)*

Rnd 5: Ch 5, [sk next sc, sl st in next sc, ch 5] around, join with sl st in same st as joining st of rnd 4. Fasten off. *(12 ch-5 sps)*

Rnd 6: With RS facing, join green with sl st in any ch-5 sp, ch 5, [sl st in next ch sp, ch 5] around, join with sl st in same ch sp as beg sl st. Fasten off. *(12 ch-5 sps)*

Rnd 7: With RS facing, join yellow with sl st in any ch-5 sp, ch 6, [sl st in next ch sp, ch 6] around, join with sl st in same ch sp as beg sl st. Fasten off. *(12 ch-6 sps)*

Joining Upper & Lower Left Wings
First Bruges Lace Band

Row 1 (WS): With white, ch 8, dc in 6th ch from hook and in each of next 2 chs, turn.

Row 2: With RS of Upper Left Wing facing, **joined lp** *(see Special Stitches)* in any ch-6 sp of Upper Left Wing, dc in each of next 3 dc, turn.

Row 3: Ch 5, dc in each of next 3 dc, turn.

Row 4: With RS of Upper Left Wing facing, joined lp in next ch-6 sp of Upper Left Wing, dc in each of next 3 dc, turn.

Row 5: Ch 5, dc in each of next 3 dc, turn.

Rows 6–9: Rep rows 4 and 5 alternately twice.

Row 10: With RS of Upper Left Wing facing, joined lp in same ch-6 sp of Upper Left Wing as joined lp of row before last, dc in each of next 3 dc, turn.

Rows 11–17: Rep rows 3 and 4 alternately, ending with row 3.

Row 18: With RS of Upper Left Wing facing, joined lp in same ch-6 sp of Upper Left Wing as joined lp of row before last, dc in each of next 3 dc, turn.

Rows 19–42: Rep rows 11–18 alternately 3 times.

Rows 43 & 44: Rep rows 3 and 4.

Rows 45–47: Ch 5, dc in each of next 3 dc, turn.

Row 48: With RS facing, joined lp in rem lp of foundation ch at base of center dc of row 1 3-dc group, dc in each of next 3 dc, turn.

Rows 49–53: Ch 5, dc in each of next 3 dc, turn.

Row 54: With RS of Lower Left Wing facing, joined lp in any ch-6 sp of Lower Left Wing, dc in each of next 3 dc, turn.

Row 55: Ch 5, dc in each of next 3 dc, turn.

Row 56: With RS of Lower Left Wing facing, joined lp in next ch-6 sp of Lower Left Wing, dc in each of next 3 dc, turn.

Rows 57 & 58: Rep rows 55 and 56.

Row 59: Ch 5, dc in each of next 3 dc, turn.

Row 60: With RS of Lower Left Wing facing, joined lp in same ch-6 sp of Lower Left Wing as joined lp of row before last, dc in each of next 3 dc, turn.

Rows 61–64: Rep rows 57–60.

Rows 65–70: Rep rows 55–60.

Rows 71–80: Rep rows 61–70.

Rows 81 & 82: Rep rows 55 and 56.

Row 83: With WS facing, joined lp in ch-5 lp of row 7, dc in each of next 3 dc, turn.

Row 84: With RS of Lower Left Wing facing, joined lp in next ch-6 sp of Lower Left Wing, dc in each of next 3 dc, turn.

Row 85: With WS facing, joined lp in ch-5 lp of row 5, dc in each of next 3 dc, turn.

Row 86: Rep row 60.

Row 87: With WS facing, joined lp in ch-5 lp of row 3, dc in each of next 3 dc, turn.

Row 88: With RS of Lower Left Wing facing, joined lp in next ch-6 sp of Lower Left Wing, dc in each of next 3 dc, turn.

Row 89: With WS facing, joined lp in ch-5 lp of row 1, sl st in ch-5 sp of row 50, dc in each of next 3 dc, ch 2, sl st in ch-5 sp of row 52. Fasten off.

Border for Left Wing

With RS facing, join rose with sl st in ch-5 sp on row 9 of First Bruges Lace Band, (ch 3, sl st) in same ch sp, ch 6, sl st in next joined lp, ch 3, sl st in next joined lp, *ch 6, (sl st, ch 3, sl st) in next lp, rep from * around, ending with ch 6, join with sl st in beg sl st. Fasten off.

Joining Left Wing to Body

With RS facing, join black with sl st in first ch-6 sp of rnd 1 of Border for Left Wing, ch 3, sl st in next ch-6 sp, ch 6, *(sl st, ch 3, sl st) in next ch-6 sp, ch 4, sl st in 2nd ch from hook for picot, ch 3*, rep between * 9 times, sl st in next ch-6 sp, ch 3, sl st in end of row 32 of Body, [ch 3, sl st in next ch-6 sp on Border, ch 3, sk next 2 rows on Body, sl st in end of next row] 9 times, ch 3, sl st in next ch-6 sp on Border, ch 4, sl st in 2nd ch from hook for picot, ch 3, rep between * around, ending with (sl st, ch 3, sl st) in last ch-6 sp, ch 6, join with sl st in beg sl st. Fasten off.

Upper Right Wing

Rnds 1–5: Rep rnds 1–5 of Upper Left Wing.

Lower Right Wing

Rnds 1–7: Rep rnds 1–7 of Lower Left Wing.

Joining Upper & Lower Right Wings
Second Bruges Lace Band

Row 1 (RS): Rep row 1 of First Bruges Lace Band.

Row 2: With WS of Upper Right Wing facing, joined lp in any ch-6 sp of Upper Right Wing, dc in each of next 3 dc, turn.

Row 3: Ch 5, dc in each of next 3 dc, turn.

Row 4: With WS of Upper Right Wing facing, joined lp in next ch-6 sp of Upper Right Wing, dc in each of next 3 dc, turn.

Row 5: Ch 5, dc in each of next 3 dc, turn.

Rows 6–9: Rep rows 4 and 5 alternately twice.

Row 10: With WS of Upper Right Wing facing, joined lp in same ch-6 sp as joined lp of row before last, dc in each of next 3 dc, turn.

Rows 11–17: Rep rows 3 and 4 alternately, ending with row 3.

Row 18: With WS of Upper Right Wing facing, joined lp in same ch-6 sp as joined lp of row before last, dc in each of next 3 dc, turn.

Rows 19–42: Rep rows 11–18 consecutively 3 times.

Rows 43 & 44: Rep rows 3 and 4.

Rows 45–47: Ch 5, dc in each of next 3 dc, turn.

Row 48: With WS facing, joined lp in rem lp of foundation ch at base of center dc of row 1 3-dc group, dc in each of next 3 dc, turn.

Rows 49–53: Ch 5, dc in each of next 3 dc, turn.

Row 54: With WS of Lower Right Wing facing, joined lp in any ch-6 lp of lower right wing, dc in each of next 3 dc, turn.

Row 55: Ch 5, dc in each of next 3 dc, turn.

Row 56: With WS of Lower Right Wing facing, joined lp in next ch-6 sp of Lower Right Wing, dc in each of next 3 dc, turn.

Rows 57 & 58: Rep rows 55 and 56.

Row 59: Ch 5, dc in each of next 3 dc, turn.

Row 60: With WS of Lower Right Wing facing, joined lp in same ch-6 sp of Lower Right Wing as joined lp of row before last, dc in each of next 3 dc, turn.

Rows 61–64: Rep rows 57–60.

Rows 65–70: Rep rows 55–60.

Rows 71–80: Rep rows 61–70.

Rows 81 & 82: Rep rows 55 and 56.

Row 83: With RS facing, joined lp in ch-5 sp of row 7, dc in each of next 3 dc, turn.

Row 84: Rep row 56.

Row 85: With RS facing, joined lp in ch-5 sp of row 5, dc in each of next 3 dc, turn.

Row 86: Rep row 60.

Row 87: With RS facing, joined lp in ch-5 sp of row 3, dc in each of next 3 dc, turn.

Row 88: Rep row 56.

Row 89: With RS facing, joined lp in ch-5 sp of row 1, sl st in ch-5 sp of row 50, dc in each of next 3 dc, ch 2, sl st in ch-5 sp of row 52. Fasten off.

Border for Right Wing

With RS facing, join rose with sl st in ch-5 sp on row 81 of Bruges Lace Band, rep Border for Left Wing.

Joining Right Wing to Body

With RS facing, join black with sl st in first ch-6 sp of Border for Right Wing, ch 3, sl st in next ch-6 sp, ch 6, *(sl st, ch 3, sl st) in next ch-6 sp, ch 4, sl st in 2nd ch from hook for picot, ch 3*, rep between * 14 times, sl st in next ch-6 sp, ch 3, sl st in end of row 5 of Body, [ch-3, sl st in next ch-6 sp on Border, ch 3, sk next 2 rows of Body, sl st in end of next row] 9 times, ch 3, sl st in next ch-6 sp on Border, ch 4, sl st in 2nd ch from hook for picot, ch 3, rep between * around, ending with (sl st, ch 3, sl st) in last ch-6 sp, ch 6, join with sl st in beg sl st. Fasten off.

Antennae

Row 1: With WS facing, join black with sl st in 4th picot from last joining of Wing and Body at top right-hand side of Butterfly Wing, ch 15, sl st in 11th unworked sc from row 1 of Body on right-hand side of rnd 2 of Head, sl st in each of next 2 sc, ch 15, sl st in corresponding picot at top left-hand side of opposite Butterfly Wing, turn.

Row 2: Ch 1, sl st in each of next 15 chs, sk next sl st, sl st in next sl st, sk next sl st, sl st in each of last 15 chs, sl st in same st on Butterfly Wing as beg of sl st of row 1. Fasten off.

NAPKIN RING

Row 1 (WS): With white, ch 8, dc in 6th ch from hook and in each of next 2 chs, turn.

Rows 2–16: Ch 5, dc in each of next 3 dc, turn. At end of last row, fasten off.

With tapestry needle, sew top of each of last 3 dc of last row to rem lp of foundation ch at base of each of 3 dc of first row.

Border
First edge

Rnd 1: With RS facing, join rose with sl st in any ch-5 sp on either edge of Napkin Ring, ch 5, [sl st in next ch-5 sp, ch 5] around, join with sl st in beg sl st. Fasten off.

Rnd 2: With RS facing, join black with sl st in any ch-5 sp, ch 5, [sl st in next ch-5 sp, ch 5] around, join with sl st in beg sl st. Fasten off.

Second edge

Rnd 1: With RS facing, join green with sl st in any ch-5 sp on other edge of Napkin Ring, ch 5, [sl st in next ch-5 sp, ch 5] around, join with sl st in beg sl st. Fasten off.

Rnd 2: With RS facing, join yellow with sl st in any ch-5 sp on, ch 5, [sl st in next ch-5 sp, ch 5] around, join with sl st in beg sl st. Fasten off.

FINISHING

Wash Place Mat and Napkin Ring. Starch lightly. When dry, steam-press Place Mat lightly on WS. ❏❏

Designs by June Hardy

OVAL MAT

SKILL LEVEL
INTERMEDIATE

FINISHED SIZE
10½ X 20 inches

MATERIALS
❑ Bulky (chunky) weight yarn:
4 oz/140yds/113g main color (MC)
1 oz/35 yds/28g contrasting color (CC)
½ oz/18 yds/14g green
❑ Size I/9/5.5mm crochet hook or size needed to obtain gauge
❑ Tapestry needle

GAUGE
3 dc = 1 inch, 3 dc rows = 2 inches

INSTRUCTIONS
MAT

Rnd 1: With MC, ch 22, 3 dc in 4th ch from hook *(first 3 chs count as first dc)* and in each ch across with 7 dc in last ch; working on opposite side of ch, dc in each ch across with 3 dc in last ch, join with sl st in 3rd ch of beg ch-3. *(48 dc)*

Rnd 2: Ch 3 *(counts as first dc throughout)*, dc in same st, 2 dc in each of next 2 sts, dc in each of next 19 sts, 2 dc in each of next 5 sts, dc in each of next 19 sts, 2 dc in each of last 2 sts, join with sl st in 3rd ch of beg ch-3. *(58 dc)*

Rnd 3: Ch 3, dc in same st, 2 dc in each of next 3 sts, dc in each of next 23 sts, 2 dc in each of next 6 sts, dc in each of next 23 sts, 2 dc in each of last 2 sts, join with sl st in 3rd ch of beg ch-3. *(70 dc)*

Rnd 4: Ch 3, dc in same st, 2 dc in each of next 5 sts, dc in each of next 27 sts, 2 dc in each of next 8 sts, dc in each of next 27 sts, 2 dc in each of last 2 sts, join with sl st in 3rd ch of beg ch-3. *(86 dc)*

Rnd 5: Ch 3, dc in same st, 2 dc in each of next 7 sts, dc in each of next 35 sts, 2 dc in each of next 8 sts, dc in each of last 35 sts, join with sl st in 3rd ch of beg ch-3. *(102 dc)*

Rnd 6: Ch 3, dc in each of next 3 sts, 2 dc in each of next 9 sts, dc in each of next 42 sts, 2 dc in each of next 9 sts, dc in each of last 38 sts, join with sl st in 3rd ch of beg ch-3, **turn.** *(120 dc)*

Rnd 7: Ch 14, sk next 7 sts, [sl st in next st, ch 14, sk next 7 sts] around, join with sl st in bottom of beg ch-14, **do not turn.** *(15 ch sps)*

Rnd 8 (RS): Sl st in next ch, ch 2 *(counts as first hdc)*, hdc in each ch and sl st in each sl st around, join with sl st in 2nd ch of beg ch-2. Fasten off.

Trim

Rnd 1: Working in unworked sts of rnd 6, behind ch sps of rnd 7, join CC with sl st in center dc between sl sts, ch 12, [sl st in center dc between sl sts, ch 12] around, join with sl st in beg sl st. *(15 ch sps)*

Rnd 2: Sl st in next ch, ch 1, sc in each ch and sl st in each sl st around, join with sl st in beg sc. Fasten off.

With green, embroider 3 lazy daisy sts (see illustration) at base of each MC ch sp as shown in photo.

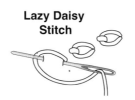

Lazy Daisy Stitch

With pink, embroider 1 French knot (see illustration), in center of each lazy daisy group as shown.

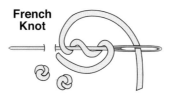

French Knot

SQUARE & ROUND MATS

SKILL LEVEL
INTERMEDIATE

FINISHED SIZES
Square Mat: 10½ inches square
Round Mat: 11 inches across

MATERIALS
❑ Bulky (chunky) weight yarn:
3 oz/105 yds/85g main color (MC)
1 oz/35 yds/28g each contrasting color (CC) and green
❑ Size I/9/5.5mm crochet hook or size needed to obtain gauge
❑ Tapestry needle

GAUGE
3 dc = 1 inch, 3 dc rows = 2 inches

INSTRUCTIONS
SQUARE MAT

Rnd 1: With MC, ch 4, sl st in first ch to form ring, ch 3 *(counts as first dc throughout)*, 2 dc in ring, ch 2, [3 dc in ring, ch 2] 3 times, join with sl st in 3rd ch of beg ch-3. *(12 dc)*

Rnd 2: Ch 3, dc in each of next 2 dc, (2 dc, ch 2, 2 dc) in next ch-2 sp, *dc in each of next 3 dc, (2 dc, ch 2, 2 dc) in next ch-2 sp, rep from * around, join with sl st in 3rd ch of beg ch-3. *(28 dc, 4 corner ch sps)*

Rnds 3–5: Ch 3, dc in each dc around with (2 dc, ch 2, 2 dc) in each corner ch-2 sp, join with sl st in 3rd ch of beg ch-3. At end of last rnd *(72 dc and 4 corner ch sps)*.

Rnd 6: Sl st in each of next 4 sts, **turn,** *ch 12, sk next 6 sts, sl st in next st, ch 12, sk next 5 sts, sl st in next ch-2 sp, ch 12, sk next 5 sts*, sl st in next st, rep between *, sl st in next st, rep between * around, join with sl st in beg sl st. *(12 ch sps)*

Rnd 7 (RS): Sl st in next ch, ch 2, hdc in each ch and sl st in each sl st around, join with sl st in 2nd ch of beg ch-2. Fasten off.

Trim

Rnd 1: Working in unworked sts of rnd 5, behind ch sps of rnd 6, join CC with sl st in center dc between sl sts, ch 10, [sl st in center dc between sl sts, ch 10] around, join with sl st in beg sl st. *(12 ch sps)*

Rnd 2: Sl st in next ch, ch 1, sc in each ch and sl st in each sl st around, join with sl st in beg sc. Fasten off. Embroider in same manner as Oval Mat.

ROUND MAT

Rnd 1: With MC, ch 6, sl st in first ch to form ring, ch 3 *(counts as first dc throughout)*, dc in same ch, 2 dc in each ch around, join with sl st in 3rd ch of beg ch-3. *(12 dc)*

Rnds 2 & 3: Ch 3, dc in same st, 2 dc in each st around, join with sl st in 3rd ch of beg ch-3. At end of last rnd. *(48 dc)*

Rnd 4: Ch 3, dc in same st, dc in each of next 2 sts, [2 dc in next st, dc in each of next 2 sts] around, join with sl st in 3rd ch of beg ch-3. *(64 dc)*

Rnd 5: Ch 3, dc in same st, dc in each of next 3 sts, [2 dc in next st, dc in each of next 3 sts] around, join with sl st in 3rd ch of beg ch-3, **turn.** *(80 dc)*

Rnd 6: Ch 12, sk next 6 sts, sl st in next st, ch 12, sk next 6 sts, [sl st in next st, ch 12, sk next 5 sts] around, join with sl st in first ch of beg ch-12. *(13 ch sps)*

Rnd 7 (RS): Sl st in next ch, ch 2 *(counts as first hdc)*, hdc in each ch and sl st in each sl st around, join with sl st in 2nd ch of beg ch-2. Fasten off.

Trim

Work in same manner as Square Mat Trim. ❑❑

Flower Coaster

Design by Judy Teague Treece

FINISHED SIZE
4¾ inches across

MATERIALS FOR ONE
- ❑ Crochet cotton size 10:
  20 yds each color A and B
- ❑ Size 6/1.80mm steel crochet hook or size needed to obtain gauge

GAUGE
Rnds 1–3 = 1¾ inches across

PATTERN NOTE
Coaster may ruffle until blocked.

SPECIAL STITCHES
Beginning shell (beg shell): Ch 3 *(counts as first dc)*, (dc, ch 2, 2 dc) in same ch sp.

Shell: (2 dc, ch 2, 2 dc) in next ch sp.

Beginning cluster (beg cl): Ch 3, [yo, insert hook in same ch sp, yo, pull lp through, yo, pull through 2 lps on hook] twice, yo, pull through all lps on hook.

Cluster (cl): Yo, insert hook in next ch sp, yo, pull lp through, yo, pull through 2 lps on hook, [yo, insert hook in same ch sp, yo, pull lp through, yo, pull through 2 lps on hook] twice, yo, pull through all lps on hook.

INSTRUCTIONS
COASTER
Rnd 1: With A, ch 5, sl st in first ch to form ring, ch 4 *(counts as first dc and ch 1)*, (dc in ring, ch 1) 7 times, join with sl st in 3rd ch of ch-4. *(8 dc, 8 ch sps)*

Rnd 2: Sl st in next ch sp, **beg shell** *(see Special Stitches)*, ch 1, [**shell** *(see Special Stitches)* in next ch sp, ch 1] around, join with sl st in 3rd ch of beg ch-3. *(8 shells, 8 ch-1 sps)*

Rnd 3: Sl st in next st, sl st in next ch sp, beg shell, ch 2, sc in next ch-1 sp, ch 2, [shell in ch sp of next shell, ch 2, sc in next ch-1 sp, ch 2] around, join with sl st in 3rd ch of beg ch-3. Fasten off. *(16 ch-2 sps, 8 shells)*

Rnd 4: Join B with sl st in first shell, (**beg cl**—*see Special Stitches*, ch 2, **cl**—*see Special Stitches*) in same shell, ch 6, sk next 2 ch-2 sps, *(cl, ch 2, cl) in next shell, ch 6, sk next 2 ch-2 sps, rep from * around, join with sl st in top of beg cl. *(16 cls, 8 ch-6 sps, 8 ch-2 sps)*

Rnd 5: Sl st in first ch sp, (beg cl, ch 2, cl, ch 2, cl) in same ch sp, ch 6, sk next ch-6 sp, *(cl, ch 2, cl, ch 2, cl) in next ch-2 sp, ch 6, sk next ch-6 sp, rep from * around, join with sl st in top of beg cl. *(24 cls)*

Rnd 6: Sl st in next ch-2 sp, beg cl, *ch 2, cl in same ch sp, ch 2, (cl, ch 2, cl) in next ch-2 sp, ch 6, sk next ch-6 sp**, cl in next ch-2 sp, rep from * around, ending last rep at **, join with sl st in top of beg cl. *(32 cls)*

Rnd 7: Sl st in next ch sp, beg cl, *ch 2, cl in same ch sp, ch 2, cl in next ch-2 sp, ch 2, (cl, ch 2, cl) in next ch-2 sp, ch 5, sc around all 3 ch-6 lps of last 3 rnds at same time, ch 5**, cl in next ch-2 sp, rep from * around, ending last rep at **, join with sl st in top of beg cl. Fasten off. *(40 cls)*

Rnd 8: Join A with sc in first ch-2 sp, *ch 2, [sc in next ch-2 sp, ch 2] 3 times, 5 sc in each of next 2 ch-5 sps, ch 2**, sc in next ch-2 sp, rep from * around, ending last rep at **, join with sl st in first sc.

Rnd 9: Sl st in next ch-2 sp, ch 1, (sc, ch 3, sc) in same ch sp, (sc, ch 3, sc) in each of next 3 ch-2 sps, *sk next st, sc in next st, ch 3, sc in next st, sl st in each of next 2 sts, sc in next st, [ch 3, sk next st, sc in next st] twice**, (sc, ch 3, sc) in each of next 5 ch-2 sps, rep from * around, ending last rep at **, (sc, ch 3, sc) in last ch-2 sp, join with sl st in beg sc. Fasten off. ❑❑

Floral Jar Covers

Design by Patricia Hall

SKILL LEVEL

■■■□

INTERMEDIATE

FINISHED SIZES

Off-White Cover: 6 inches across
Light Yellow Cover: 6 inches across
White Cover: 6¾ inches across

MATERIALS

- ❑ Medium (worsted) weight yarn:
  1 oz/50 yds/28g each
  off-white, light yellow
  and white
- ❑ Crochet cotton size 10:
  42 yds avocado
  21 yds purple
  16 yds red
  10 yds orange
  3 yds yellow
- ❑ Size 4 steel crochet hook
- ❑ Size G crochet hook or sizes
  needed to obtain gauge
- ❑ Tapestry needle
- ❑ 24 inches each off-white, orange
  and white ⅝-inch-wide satin ribbon

GAUGE

Size G hook: Rnds 1–3 of Top =
3½ inches across
Size 4 steel hook: Red Flower =
1¾ inches across, Orange Flower =
1½ inches across, Purple Flower =
1¼ inches across

PATTERN NOTES

Use size G hook with medium weight
yarn.

Use size 4 steel hook with crochet cotton.

SPECIAL STITCHES

**Beginning treble crochet cluster
(beg tr cl):** Ch 3, *yo twice, insert
hook in same st, yo, pull lp through,
[yo, pull through 2 lps on hook]
twice, rep from *, yo, pull through
all lps on hook.

Treble crochet cluster (tr cl): Yo
twice, *insert hook in next st, yo, pull
lp through, [yo, pull through 2 lps on

hook] twice, rep from * twice
st, yo, pull through all lps o

Picot: Ch 4, sl st in top of st

**Beginning double treble crochet
cluster (beg dtr cl):** Ch 4, *yo 3
times, insert hook in same st, yo, pull
lp through, [yo, pull through 2 lps
on hook] 3 times; rep from * twice,
yo, pull through all lps on hook.

**Double treble crochet cluster
(dtr cl):** Yo 3 times, *insert hook in
next st, yo, pull lp through, [yo, pull
through 2 lps on hook] 3 times; rep
from * 3 more times in same st, yo,
pull through all lps on hook.

INSTRUCTIONS
OFF-WHITE COVER
Top

Rnd 1: With G hook and off-white, ch
4, 11 dc in 4th ch from hook *(first 3
chs count as first dc)*, join with sl st
in 3rd ch of ch-3. *(12 dc)*

ds 2 & 3: Ch 3 *(counts as first dc
throughout)*, dc in same st, 2 dc in
each st around, join with sl st in 3rd
ch of beg ch-3. *(24 dc, 48 dc)*

Rnd 4: Working this rnd in **back lps**
(see Stitch Guide) only, ch 4 *(counts
as first dc and ch-1)*, sk next st, [dc
in next st, ch 1, sk next st] around,
join with sl st in 3rd ch of beg ch-4.
(24 dc, 24 ch-1 sps)

Rnd 5: Ch 1, sc in each st and in
each ch around, join with sl st in
beg sc. *(48 sc)*

Rnd 6: (Beg tr cl—*see Special Stitches*,
ch 9, **tr cl**—*see Special Stitches)*, in
next st, sk next 2 sts, [tr cl in next
st, ch 9, tr cl in next st, sk next 2 sts]
around, join with sl st in top of beg tr
cl. Fasten off. *(24 tr-cls, 12 ch sps)*

Rnd 7: For **edging,** with size 4 hook
and red, join with sc in sp between
last and first tr cls, ch 7, (sc, hdc, dc,
tr, **picot**—*see Special Stitches*, tr, dc,
hdc, sc) in next ch sp, ch 7, *sc in sp
between next 2 tr-cls, ch 7, (sc, hdc,
dc, tr, picot, tr, dc, hdc, sc) in next

ch sp, ch 7, rep from * around, join with sl st in beg sc. Fasten off.

Leaves
Rnd 1: With size 4 steel hook and avocado, ch 12, sl st in first ch to form ring, ch 3, 23 dc in ring, join with sl st in 3rd ch of beg ch-3. *(24 dc)*

Rnd 2: Ch 1, sc in first st, [ch 5, sk next st, sc in next st] around, join with ch 2, sk last st, dc in first sc forming last ch sp. *(12 sc, 12 ch sps)*

Rnd 3: Ch 1, sc around ch sp just made, [ch 5, sc in next ch sp] around; join with ch 2, dc in first sc forming last ch sp.

Rnd 4: Ch 1, sc in ch sp just made, ch 5, [sc in next ch lp, ch 5] around, join with sl st in beg sc.

Rnd 5: Beg dtr cl *(see Special Stitches)*, ch 6, sc in next ch sp, ch 6, [**dtr cl** *(see Special Stitches)* in next sc, ch 6, sc in next ch sp, ch 6] around, join with sl st in top of beg dtr cl. Fasten off.

Tack over rnds 1–3 of Top.

Red Flower
Rnd 1: With size 4 steel hook and red, ch 6, sl st in first ch to form ring, ch 3, 23 dc in ring, join with sl st in top of ch-3. *(24 dc)*

Rnd 2: Ch 6, sk next 7 sts, [sl st in next st, ch 6, sk next 7 sts] around, join with sl st in first ch of first beg ch-6. *(3 ch sps)*

Rnd 3: Sl st in first ch sp, ch 1, (sc, hdc, dc, 5 tr, dc, hdc, sc) in same ch sp and in each ch sp around, join with sl st in beg sc. Fasten off.

Rnd 4: Fold petals forward, join with sl st in 4th dc of any sk 7-dc group on rnd 1, ch 6, [sl st in 4th dc on next sk 7-dc group, ch 6] around, join with sl st in beg sl st. *(3 ch sps)*

Rnd 5: Rep rnd 3.

Rnd 6: Fold petals forward, join with sl st in 2nd dc of any sk 3-dc group on rnd 1, ch 6, sk next 3-dc group, [sl st in 2nd dc of next sk 3-dc group, ch 6, sk next 3-dc group] around, join with sl st in beg sl st.

Rnd 7: Sl st in first ch sp, (sc, ch 2, 2 tr, 10 dtr, 2 tr, ch 2, sc) in same ch and in each ch sp around, join with sl st in beg sl st. Fasten off.

For **center of flower,** with size 4 steel hook and yellow, ch 3, (2 dc, sl st) in 3rd ch from hook. Fasten off. Tack to center of flower.

Tack red flower to center of Leaves.

Weave off-white ribbon through ch sps of rnd 4 on Top. Tie ends into a bow.

LIGHT YELLOW COVER
Top
Rnd 1: With size G hook and light yellow, ch 4, 11 dc in 4th ch from hook *(first 3 chs count as first dc)*, join with sl st in 3rd ch of ch-3. *(12 dc)*

Rnds 2 & 3: Ch 3 *(counts as first dc throughout)*, dc in same st, 2 dc in each st around, join with sl st in 3rd ch of beg ch-3. *(24 dc, 48 dc)*

Rnd 4: Working this rnd in back lps only, ch 4 *(counts as first dc and ch-1)*, sk next st, [dc in next st, ch 1, sk next st] around, join with sl st in 3rd ch of beg ch-4. *(24 dc, 24 ch-1 sps)*

Rnd 5: Ch 1, sc in each st and in each ch around, join with sl st in beg sc. *(48 sc)*

Rnd 6: Ch 1, sc in first st, ch 6, sk next st, tr cl in next st, ch 8, tr cl in next st, ch 6, sk next 2 sts, *sc in next st, ch 6, sk next 2 sts, tr cl in next st, ch 8, tr cl in next st, ch 6, sk next 2 sts, rep from * around, join with sl st in beg sc. Fasten off *(14 tr-cls, 14 ch-6 sps, 7 sc, 7 ch-8 sps)*

Rnd 7: With size 4 steel hook and orange, join with sc in first sc, ch 10, 2 sc in next tr cl, ch 14, 2 sc in next tr cl, ch 10, *sc in next sc, ch 10, 2 sc in next tr cl, ch 14, 2 sc in next tr cl, ch 10, rep from * around, join with sl st in beg sc. Fasten off.

Leaves
Rnd 1: With size 4 steel hook and avocado, ch 12, sl st in first ch to form ring, ch 3, 23 dc in ring, join with sl st in 3rd ch of beg ch-3. *(24 dc)*

Rnd 2: Ch 1, sc in first st, [ch 5, sk next st, sc in next st] around, joining with ch 2, sk last st, dc in first sc forming last ch sp. *(12 sc, 12 ch sps)*

Rnd 3: Ch 1, sc in ch sp just made, ch 11, [sc in next ch sp, ch 11] around, join with sl st in beg sc.

Rnd 4: Ch 1, *sc in next st, ch 6, (sc, ch 4, sc) in next ch sp, ch 6, rep from * around, join with sl st in beg sc. Fasten off.

Tack Leaves over rnds 1–3 on Top.

Orange Flower
Rnd 1: With size 4 steel hook and orange, ch 5, sl st in first ch to form ring, ch 2 *(counts as first hdc throughout)*, 13 hdc in ring, join with sl st in 2nd ch of beg ch-2. *(14 hdc)*

Rnd 2: Ch 3, sk next st, [sl st in next st, ch 3, sk next st] around, join with sl st in first ch of beg ch-3. *(7 ch sps)*

Rnd 3: (Sl st, ch 2, 2 dc, ch 2, sl st) in each ch sp around, join with sl st in beg sl st. Fasten off.

Rnd 4: Fold petal forward, join with sl st in any sk st on rnd 1, ch 4, [sl st in next sk st, ch 4] around, join with sl st in beg sl st.

Rnd 5: Sl st in first ch sp, ch 1 (sc, ch 1, dc, 3 tr, dc, ch 1, sc) in same ch sp and in each ch sp around, join with sl st in beg sc. Fasten off.

For **center of flower,** with size 4 hook and yellow, ch 3, (2 dc, sl st) in 3rd ch from hook. Fasten off. Tack to center of flower.

Tack orange flower to center of Leaves.

Weave orange ribbon through ch sps of rnd 4 on Top. Tie ends into a bow.

WHITE COVER
Rnd 1: With size G hook and white, ch 4, 11 dc in 4th ch from hook *(first 3 chs count as first dc)*, join with sl st in 3rd ch of ch-3. *(12 dc)*

Rnds 2 & 3: Ch 3 *(counts as first dc throughout)*, dc in same st, 2 dc in each st around, join with sl st in 3rd ch of beg ch-3. *(24 dc, 48 dc)*

Rnd 4: Working this rnd in back lps only, ch 4 *(counts as first dc and ch-1)*, sk next st, [dc in next st, ch 1, sk next st] around, join with sl st in 3rd ch of beg ch-4. *(24 dc, 24 ch-1 sps)*

Rnd 5: Ch 1, sc in each st and in each ch around, join with sl st in beg sc. *(48 sc)*

Rnd 6: Ch 1, sc in first st, ch 9, sk next 3 sts, [sc in next st, ch 9, sk next 3 sts] around, join with sl st in beg sc. *(12 sc, 12 ch-9 sps)*

Rnd 7: Ch 1, sc in first st, (5 dc, ch 2, sc, ch 2, 5 dc) in next ch sp, *sc in next sc, (5 dc, ch 2, sc, ch 2, 5 dc) in next ch sp, rep from * around, join with sl st in beg sc. Fasten off. *(120 dc, 24 ch-2 sps, 24 sc)*

Rnd 8: With size 4 steel hook and purple, join with sc in first sc, *[ch 9, sk next 4 dc, sc in next dc, ch 5, (sc, ch 4, sc) in next sc, ch 5, sc in next dc, ch 9, sk next 4 dc**, sc in next sc, rep from * around, ending last rep at **, join with sl st in beg sc. Fasten off.

Leaves
Rnd 1: With size 4 steel hook and avocado, ch 12, sl st in first ch to form ring, ch 3, 23 dc in ring, join with sl st in 3rd ch of beg ch-3. *(24 dc)*

Rnd 2: Ch 1, sc in first st, [ch 4, sk next st, sc in next st] around, joining with ch 2, sk last st, dc in first sc forming last ch sp. *(12 sc, 12 ch sps)*

Rnd 3: Ch 1, sc in ch sp just made, [ch 5, sc in next ch sp] around; joining with ch 2, dc in first sc forming last ch sp.

Rnd 4: Ch 1, sc in ch sp just made, ch 7, [sc in next ch sp, ch 7] around, join with sl st in beg sc.

Rnd 5: Sl st in first ch sp, ch 1, (sc, hdc, dc, 2 tr, **picot**—*see Special Stitches*, tr, dc, hdc, sc) in same ch sp and in each ch sp around, join with sl st in beg sc. Fasten off.
Tack over rnds 1–3 of Top.

Purple Flower
Make 3.
Rnd 1: With size 4 hook and purple, ch 5, sl st in first ch to form ring, ch 2 *(counts as first hdc throughout)*, 9 hdc in ring, join with sl st in 2nd ch of beg ch-2. *(10 hdc)*

Rnd 2: ◊Ch 4, *yo twice, insert hook in same st, yo, pull lp through, [yo, pull through 2 lps on hook] twice*, rep between *, yo twice, insert hook in next st, yo, pull lp through, [yo, pull through 2 lps on hook] twice, rep between *, yo, pull through all lps on hook, ch 4, sl st in same st◊, [sl st in next st, rep between ◊] around, join with sl st in beg sl st. Fasten off.

For **center of flower** *(make 3)*, with size 4 hook and yellow, ch 3, (2 dc, sl st) in 3rd ch from hook. Fasten off. Tack to center of each flower.

Tack purple flowers to rnds 1–3 of Leaves.

Weave white ribbon through ch sps of rnd 4 on Top. Tie ends into a bow. ❑❑

Checkered Hot Mats
Designs by Vicki Blizzard

SKILL LEVEL
INTERMEDIATE

FINISHED SIZE
10½ inches square

MATERIALS
❑ Red Heart Classic medium (worsted) weight yarn (3½ oz/198 yds/99g per skein):
  2 skeins #1 white
  1 skein each #686 paddy green and #902 jockey red
  ½ skein #230 yellow
❑ Size G/6/4mm crochet hook or size needed to obtain gauge
❑ Tapestry needle

GAUGE
18 sc = 5 inches, 19 sc rows = 5 inches

PATTERN NOTES
Change color *(see Stitch Guide)* in last stitch made.

Carry color not in use loosely across back of work until needed again; do not work over color not in use.

SPECIAL STITCH
Picot: Ch 3, sl st in 3rd ch from hook.

INSTRUCTIONS
POINSETTIA HOT MAT
First Side
Row 1 (RS): With white, ch 33, sc in 2nd ch from hook, sc in each of next 3 chs, changing to paddy green in last st (see Pattern Notes), *sc in each of next 4 chs**, changing to white in last st, sc in each of next 4 sts, changing to paddy green in last st, rep from * across, ending last rep at **, do not change to A, turn. (32 sc)

Row 2: Matching colors on working row to colors on previous row, ch 1, sc in each sc across, turn.

Rows 3 & 4: Rep row 2, changing to paddy green at end of last row.

Row 5: Working paddy green over white and white over paddy green, ch 1, sc in each sc across, turn.

Rows 6–8: Rep row 2, changing to white at end of last row.

Rows 9–32: Work even on 32 sc in established check pattern. At end of last row, fasten off.

Second Side
Rows 1–32: Rep rows 1–32 of First Side.

Poinsettia
Rnd 1: With yellow, ch 4, sl st in first ch to form ring, ch 1, 8 sc in ring, join with sl st in beg sc. Fasten off.

Rnd 2: Join jockey red with sl st in **back lp** (see Stitch Guide) only of any sc of last rnd, [ch 8, sc in 2nd ch from hook, hdc in next ch, dc in next ch, tr in next ch, dc in next ch, hdc in next ch, sc in last ch, sl st in back lp only of next sc on rnd 1] around. Leaving 18-inch end for sewing, fasten off.

With tapestry needle, sew poinsettia to bottom left corner of First Side.

Border
Rnd 1: With WS of First and Second Sides tog, working through both thicknesses, join jockey red with sl st in upper right corner, ch 1, sc in same st, sc in each st across to next corner, 4 sc in corner st, sc evenly sp in end of rows to next corner, 4 sc in corner st, working in starting ch on opposite side of row 1, sc in each ch across to next corner, 4 sc in corner st, sc evenly sp in end of rows to next corner, 2 sc in same st as beg sc, ch 8 for hanging lp, sc in same st as last 2 sc, join with sl st in beg sc. Fasten off.

Rnd 2: Join white with sl st in back lp only of last sc of last rnd, ch 3 (counts as first dc), working in back lps only, 4 dc in same st, *sk next st, sc in next st, sk next st, 5 dc in next st, rep from *around, working behind hanging lp and adjusting number of sts sk at end of rnd, if necessary, so pattern rep comes out even, join with sl st in beg sc. Fasten off.

HOLLY BERRY HOT MAT
First Side
Rows 1–32: Rep rows 1–32 of First Side for Poinsettia Hot Mat, substituting jockey red for paddy green.

Second Side
Rows 1–32: Rep rows 1–32 of Second Side for Poinsettia Hot Mat, substituting jockey red for paddy green.

Holly Leaf
Make 2.
With paddy green, ch 10, sc in 2nd ch from hook, *hdc in next ch, dc in next ch, **picot** (see Special Stitch), dc in next ch, hdc in next ch, dc in next ch, picot, dc in next ch, hdc in next ch*, 3 sc in last ch, working across opposite side of ch, rep between *, sc in last ch. Leaving an 18-inch end for sewing, fasten off.

Holly Berry
Make 3.
With jockey red, ch 4, sl st in first ch to form a ring, ch 1, 6 sc in ring, join with sl st in beg sc. Leaving 12-inch end for sewing, fasten off. With tapestry needle, sew Holly Leaves and Berries to bottom left corner of First Side as shown in photo.

Border
Rnd 1: With WS of First and Second Sides tog, working through both thicknesses, join paddy green with sl st in upper right corner, ch 1, sc in same st, sc in each st across to next corner, 4 sc in corner st, sc evenly sp in end of rows to next corner, 4 sc in corner st, working in starting ch on opposite side of row 1, sc in each ch across to next corner, 4 sc in corner st, sc evenly sp in end of rows to next corner, 2 sc in same st as beg sc, ch 8 for hanging lp, sc in same st as last 2 sc, join with sl st in beg sc. Fasten off.

Rnd 2: Join white with sl st in back lp only of last sc of last rnd, ch 3 (counts as first dc), working in back lps only, 4 dc in same st, *sk next st, sc in next st, sk next st, 5 dc in next st, rep from *around, working behind hanging lp and adjusting number of sts sk at end of rnd, if necessary, so pattern rep comes out even, join with sl st in beg sc. Fasten off. ❏❏

Loves Me, Loves Me Not

Designs by Maggie Petsch

SKILL LEVEL

BEGINNER

FINISHED SIZES

Place Mat: 11½ x 16 inches including Border

Napkin Ring: 1½ inches in diameter x 2 inches wide including Border

MATERIALS

❑ Crochet cotton size 3 (100 yds per ball):
    1 ball white
    61 yds red
    50 yds each green
       and yellow
❑ Crochet cotton size 10 (150 yds per ball):
    75 yds each white, yellow
      and red

❑ Size D/3/3.25mm crochet hook or size needed to obtain gauge
❑ Size 7/1.65mm steel crochet hook
❑ Tapestry needle
❑ Sewing needle
❑ Red and white sewing thread
❑ Safety pin or other marker

GAUGE

Size D hook: 16 sc = 3 inches, 18 sc rows = 3 inches

PATTERN NOTES

Change color *(see Stitch Guide)* always in last stitch made. Drop working color to wrong side.

To join with next color, insert hook in indicated stitch, yarn over with next color, complete slip stitch.

Use size D hook and size 3 crochet cotton for all Blocks.

Use size 7 steel hook and size 10 crochet cotton for Hearts and Daisies.

INSTRUCTIONS

PLACE MAT

CC Block

Make 3 each green, yellow & red in size 3 cotton.

Row 1 (RS): With size D hook, ch 17, sc in 2nd ch from hook and in each ch across, turn. *(16 sc)*

Rows 2–16: Ch 1, sc in each sc across, turn. *(16 sc)*

Rnd 17: Ch 1, sc in each sc across to last sc of last row, 3 sc in last st, *work 14 sc evenly sp in ends of rows across to next corner*, working in starting ch on opposite side of row

1, 3 sc in first ch, sc in each of next 14 chs, 3 sc in last ch, rep between *, 2 sc in same st as beg sc, join with sl st in beg sc. Fasten off.

MC Block
Make 3 white in size 3 cotton.
Row 1 (RS): With size D hook, ch 17, sc in 2nd ch from hook and in each ch across, turn. *(16 sc)*
Rows 2–16: Ch 1, sc in each sc across, turn.
Rnd 17: Ch 1, sc in each sc across to last sc of last row, 3 sc in last st, *work 14 sc evenly sp in ends of rows across to next corner*, working in starting ch on opposite side of row 1, 3 sc in first ch, sc in each of next 14 chs, 3 sc in last ch, rep between *, 2 sc in same st as beg sc, join with sl st in beg sc. Fasten off.

Border & Joining
Block 1
With size D hook and RS facing, join white with sl st in first sc to the right of corner sc in upper left corner of block 1 on joining diagram, *ch 7, sk corner sc, sl st in next sc, [ch 5, sk next 2 sc, sl st in next sc] 5 times, rep from * around, ending with last sl st in same st as beg sl st. Fasten off.

Block 2
With size D hook and RS facing, join white with sl st in first sc to the right of corner sc in upper left corner of block 2 on joining diagram, *ch 3, sl st in corresponding corner ch-7 sp on previous Block, ch 3, sk corner sc on working block, sl st in next sc*, [ch 2, sl st in next ch-5 sp on previous Block, ch 2, sk next 2 sc on working block, sl st in next sc] 5 times, rep between * *(1 side joined)*, continue around as for Border for Block 1.

Remaining Blocks
Following joining diagram for color placement, join rem blocks as for Block 2, joining as many sides as are indicated on joining diagram.

Daisy
Make 6.
Rnd 1: With size 7 steel hook and yellow size 10 crochet cotton, ch 2, 7 sc in 2nd ch from hook; **do not**

join; mark first st of rnd with safety pin or other small marker. *(7 sc)*
Rnd 2: 2 sc in each sc around, join with sl st in beg sc with white. *(14 sc)*
Rnd 3: [Ch 8, sc in 2nd ch from hook, dc in each of next 6 chs, sk next st on last rnd, sl st in next st] 7 times. Fasten off. *(7 petals)*

Heart
Make 3 each white & red.
Dc ch: With size 7 steel hook, [ch 5, dc in 5th ch from hook] 14 times. Fasten off.

Finishing
1. With sewing needle and white sewing thread, sew Daisy to center of Blocks 1, 3, 6, 8, 9 and 11 *(see Diagram)*.
2. Sew red dc chs on MC Blocks in heart shape; sew white dc chs on red Blocks in heart shape.
3. Wash Place Mat; starch lightly. Pin out to dry.

NAPKIN RING
Cut 36-inch length of red size 3 crochet cotton and set aside.
Row 1 (RS): With size D hook and size 3 white crochet cotton, ch 9, sc in 2nd ch from hook and in each ch across, turn. *(8 sc)*
Rows 2–6: Ch 1, sc in each sc across, turn. At end of last row, change to red. Fasten off white.
Row 7: Ch 1, sc in each sc across, turn.
Row 8: Ch 1, sc in first sc changing to white, sc in each of next 6 sts changing to 36-inch length of red in 6th white sc, sc in last st with red, turn.
Rows 9–13: Ch 1, sc in first st changing to white, sc in each of next 6 sts

changing to red, sc in last st, turn. At end of last row, fasten off white.
Row 14: Ch 1, sc in each sc across, changing to yellow in last st, turn. Fasten off red.
Rows 15–22: Ch 1, sc in each sc across, turn. At end of last row, change to red in last st, turn. Fasten off yellow.
Rows 23–30: Rep rows 15–22. At end of last row, change to white, turn. Fasten off red.
Rows 31 & 32: Ch 1, sc in each sc across, turn. At end of last row; fasten off.
With WS on inside, using tapestry needle, sew top of last row to bottom of row 1.

Border
First Edge
With RS facing, using size D hook, join white with sl st over in end of row 1 along either edge, ch 6, [sk next 3 rows, sl st in end of next row, ch 6] around, ending with sk last 3 rows, join with sl st in end of same row as beg sl st. Fasten off.

Second Edge
Rep instructions for First Edge on opposite edge.

Daisy
Rnds 1–3: Rep rnds 1–3 of Daisy for Place Mat.

Finishing
With sewing needle and white thread, sew center of Daisy over seam on Napkin Ring.
Wash and starch Napkin Ring lightly ❑❑

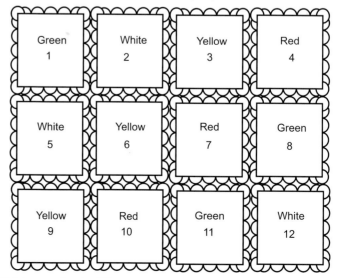

Halloween Jar Covers

Designs by Angela Tate

SKILL LEVEL

■□□□

BEGINNER

FINISHED SIZE
Fits 3-inch lid

MATERIALS
- ❏ Crochet cotton size 10:
  - 150 yds each orange and ecru
  - Small amount each white, green and black
- ❏ Size 7/1.65mm steel hook or size needed to obtain gauge
- ❏ Tapestry needle
- ❏ ⅛-inch-wide satin ribbon:
  - 20 inches orange
  - 40 inches black
- ❏ 2 sets 6mm wiggle eyes
- ❏ Black plastic spider
- ❏ Glue gun

GAUGE
5 dc = ½ inch; 2 dc rnds = ½ inch

BASIC ░░CTIONS

Rnd 1: C░░ ░░░ from hook *(first 3 c░░ ░░ join with sl st in 4t░ ░░░. (12 dc)*

Rnd 2: Ch 3 ░░ *s as first dc)*, dc in same st, 3 d░ ░░ ░ in next st, 3 dc in ░ ░░in with sl st in 3r░ ░ ░ *(30 dc)*

Rnd 3: Ch ░░ ░░░ ░, 2 dc in next dc, ░░ ░░ 2 dc, 2 dc in next c░ ░░ vith sl st in 3rd ch ░ ░ ░ dc)*

Rnd 4: C░ ░ t dc, [dc in next dc, 2 dc in ░░░ dc] around, join with sl st in 3rd ch of beg ch-3. *(60 dc)*

Rnd 5: Ch 3, dc in next dc, 2 dc in next dc, [dc in each next 2 dc, 2 dc in next dc] around, join with sl st in 3rd ch of beg ch-3. *(80 dc)*

Rnds 6–9: Ch 3, dc in each dc around, join with sl st in 3rd ch of beg ch-3.

Rnd 10: Ch 3, dc in next 2 dc, ch 1, sk next dc, [dc in each of next 3 dc, ch 1, sk next dc] around, join with sl st in 3rd ch of beg ch-3. Fasten off.

Tie
Cut a 20-inch length of satin ribbon. Weave ribbon through ch-1 sps of rnd 10.

CAT JAR COVER
Make Basic Cover with orange and a black tie.

Head
Rnd 1: With black, ch 4, 11 dc in 4th ch from hook *(first 3 chs count as first dc)*, join with sl st in 4th ch of beg ch-4. *(12 dc)*

Rnd 2: Ch 3 *(counts as first dc)*, dc in same st, 3 dc in next st, [2 dc in next st, 3 dc in next st] around, join with sl st in 3rd ch of beg ch-3. *(30 dc)*

Rnd 3: Ch 3, dc in next dc, 2 dc in next dc, [dc in each next 2 dc, 2 dc in next dc] around, join with sl st in 3rd ch of beg ch-3. *(40 dc)*

Ears
Row 4: *Ch 5, 3 dtr in same st as beg ch-5, sk next 2 dc*, sl st in each of next 5 dc, rep between *, sl st in next dc leaving rem sts unworked. Fasten off.

Facial Features
With tapestry needle and length of

white cotton, embroider smiling mouth with ch sts as shown in photo. Cut 3 strands of white cotton each 2 inches long; tie tog at center with overhand knot. Glue in place at center of Head. Glue eyes in place.

Glue Head to center of Cover.

PUMPKIN COVER

Make Basic Cover with ecru and an orange tie.

Pumpkin

Rnd 1: With orange, ch 4, 11 dc in 4th ch from hook *(first 3 chs count as first dc)*, join with sl st in 4th ch of beg ch-4. *(12 dc)*

Rnd 2: Ch 3 *(counts as first dc)*, dc in same st, 3 dc in next st, [2 dc in next st, 3 dc in next st] around, join with sl st in 3rd ch of beg ch-3. *(30 dc)*

Rnd 3: Ch 3, dc in next dc, 2 dc in next dc, [dc in each of next 2 dc, 2 dc in next dc] 7 times, changing to green in last dc *(see Stitch Guide)*, [dc in each of next 2 dc, 2 dc in next dc] twice, join with sl st in 3rd ch of beg ch-3, **turn.** *(40 dc)*

Stem

Row 4: Sl st in each of first 5 green dc, ch 6, sc in 2nd ch from hook, sc in each next 4 chs, sl st in same dc as last sl st, sl st in each rem green dc. Fasten off.

Facial Features

With tapestry needle and length of black cotton, embroider triangle-shaped nose over lower section of rnd 1 and embroider smiling mouth between rnds 2 and 3, centered below nose as shown in photo. Glue eyes in place.

Glue Pumpkin to center of Cover.

SPIDERWEB COVER

Make Basic Cover with orange and a black tie.

Spiderweb

Rnd 1: With white, ch 5, sl st in first ch to form ring, ch 5 *(counts as first dc and ch 2)*, [dc in ring, ch 2] 5 times, join with sl st in 3rd ch of beg ch-5. *(6 ch-2 sps)*

Rnd 2: Ch 9 *(counts as first dc and ch 6)*, [dc in next dc, ch 6] 5 times, join with sl st in 3rd ch of beg ch-9.

Rnd 3: Ch 7 *(counts as first dc and ch 4)*, dc in next ch-6 sp, ch 4, [dc in next dc, ch 4, dc in next ch-6 sp, ch 4] 5 times, join with sl st in 3rd ch of beg ch-7. *(12 ch-4 sps)*

Rnd 4: Ch 8 *(counts as first dc and ch 5)*, [dc in next dc, ch 5] 5 times, join with sl st in 3rd ch of beg ch-8.

Rnd 5: Ch 10 *(counts as first dc and ch 7)*, [dc in next dc, ch 7] 5 times, join with sl st in 3rd ch of beg ch-10. Fasten off.

Finishing

Glue Spiderweb to center top of Cover. Glue spider to Spiderweb. ❑❑

Stitch Guide

ABBREVIATIONS

beg	begin/beginning
bpdc	back post double crochet
bpsc	back post single crochet
bptr	back post treble crochet
CC	contrasting color
ch	chain stitch
ch-	refers to chain or space previously made (i.e. ch-1 space)
ch sp	chain space
cl	cluster
cm	centimeter(s)
dc	double crochet
dec	decrease/decreases/decreasing
dtr	double treble crochet
fpdc	front post double crochet
fpsc	front post single crochet
fptr	front post treble crochet
g	gram(s)
hdc	half double crochet
inc	increase/increases/increasing
lp(s)	loop(s)
MC	main color
mm	millimeter(s)
oz	ounce(s)
pc	popcorn
rem	remain/remaining
rep	repeat(s)
rnd(s)	round(s)
RS	right side
sc	single crochet
sk	skip(ped)
sl st	slip stitch
sp(s)	space(s)
st(s)	stitch(es)
tog	together
tr	treble crochet
trtr	triple treble
WS	wrong side
yd(s)	yard(s)
yo	yarn over

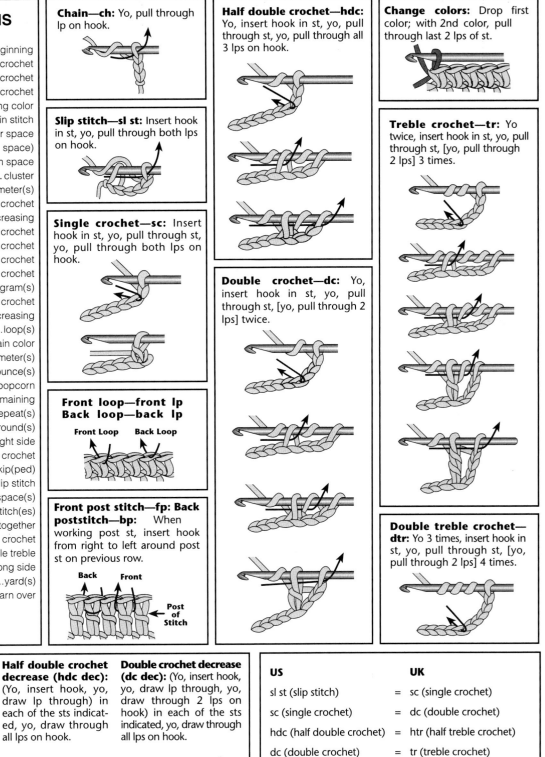

Chain—ch: Yo, pull through lp on hook.

Slip stitch—sl st: Insert hook in st, yo, pull through both lps on hook.

Single crochet—sc: Insert hook in st, yo, pull through st, yo, pull through both lps on hook.

Front loop—front lp
Back loop—back lp

Front Loop   Back Loop

Front post stitch—fp: Back poststitch—bp: When working post st, insert hook from right to left around post st on previous row.

Back   Front

Post of Stitch

Half double crochet—hdc: Yo, insert hook in st, yo, pull through st, yo, pull through all 3 lps on hook.

Double crochet—dc: Yo, insert hook in st, yo, pull through st, [yo, pull through 2 lps] twice.

Change colors: Drop first color; with 2nd color, pull through last 2 lps of st.

Treble crochet—tr: Yo twice, insert hook in st, yo, pull through st, [yo, pull through 2 lps] 3 times.

Double treble crochet—dtr: Yo 3 times, insert hook in st, yo, pull through st, [yo, pull through 2 lps] 4 times.

Single crochet decrease (sc dec): (Insert hook, yo, draw up a lp) in each of the sts indicated, yo, draw through all lps on hook.

Example of 2-sc dec

Half double crochet decrease (hdc dec): (Yo, insert hook, yo, draw lp through) in each of the sts indicated, yo, draw through all lps on hook.

Example of 2-hdc dec

Double crochet decrease (dc dec): (Yo, insert hook, yo, draw lp through, yo, draw through 2 lps on hook) in each of the sts indicated, yo, draw through all lps on hook.

Example of 2-dc dec

US		UK
sl st (slip stitch)	=	sc (single crochet)
sc (single crochet)	=	dc (double crochet)
hdc (half double crochet)	=	htr (half treble crochet)
dc (double crochet)	=	tr (treble crochet)
tr (treble crochet)	=	dtr (double treble crochet)
dtr (double treble crochet)	=	ttr (triple treble crochet)
skip	=	miss

For more complete information, visit

StitchGuide.com

306 East Parr Road
Berne, IN 46711
© 2005 Annie's Attic

TOLL-FREE ORDER LINE or to request a free catalog (800) LV-ANNIE (800) 582-6643
Customer Service (800) AT-ANNIE (800) 282-6643, **Fax** (800) 882-6643
Visit www.AnniesAttic.com

ISBN: 1-59635-039-3
Printed in USA
2 3 4 5 6 7 8 9